The Collected Works of
Langston Hughes

Volume 1

The Poems: 1921–1940

Projected Volumes in the Collected Works

The Poems: 1921–1940

The Poems: 1941–1950

The Poems: 1951–1967

The Novels: *Not without Laughter*
 and *Tambourines to Glory*

The Plays to 1942: *Mulatto* to *The Sun Do Move*

The Gospel Plays, Operas, and Other
 Late Dramatic Work

The Early Simple Stories

The Later Simple Stories

The Essays

Fight for Freedom and Related Writing

Works for Children and Young Adults: Poetry,
 Fiction, and Other Writing

Works for Children and Young Adults: Biographies

Autobiography: *The Big Sea*

Autobiography: *I Wonder as I Wander*

The Short Stories

The Translations

The Sweet Flypaper of Life

An Annotated Bibliography of the
 Works of Langston Hughes

The Collected Works of
Langston Hughes

Volume 1

The Poems: 1921–1940

Edited with an Introduction
by Arnold Rampersad

University of Missouri Press
Columbia and London

Copyright © 2001 by Ramona Bass and Arnold Rampersad, Administrators
   of the Estate of Langston Hughes
Introduction and Chronology copyright © 2001 by Arnold Rampersad
University of Missouri Press, Columbia, Missouri 65201
Printed and bound in the United States of America
All rights reserved
5 4 3 2 1   05 04 03 02 01

Library of Congress Cataloging-in-Publication Data

Hughes, Langston, 1902–1967.
   [Works. 2001]
   The collected works of Langston Hughes / edited with an introduction
      by Arnold Rampersad.
        p.   cm.
   Includes bibliographical references and index.
   Contents: v. 1. The poems, 1921–1940–
   ISBN 0-8262-1339-1 (v. 1 : alk. paper)
      1. Afro-Americans—Literary collections. I. Rampersad, Arnold. II. Title.
PS3515 .U274   2001
818'.5209—dc21   00-066601

⊚ This paper meets the requirements of the
American National Standard for Permanence of Paper
for Printed Library Materials, Z39.48, 1984.

Designer: Kristie Lee
Typesetter: BOOKCOMP, Inc.
Printer and binder: Thomson-Shore, Inc.
Typefaces: Galliard and Optima

Contents

Acknowledgments

The University of Missouri Press is grateful for assistance from the following individuals and institutions in locating and making available copies of the original editions used in the preparation of this edition: David Roessel; Anne Barker and June DeWeese, Ellis Library, University of Missouri–Columbia; Teresa Gipson, Miller Nichols Library, University of Missouri–Kansas City; Ruth Carruth and Patricia C. Willis, Beinecke Rare Book and Manuscript Library, Yale University; Ann Pathega, Washington University.

The *Collected Works* would not have been possible without the support and assistance of Patricia Powell, Chris Byrne, and Wendy Schmalz of Harold Ober Associates, representing the estate of Langston Hughes; of Judith Jones of Alfred A. Knopf, Inc.; and of Arnold Rampersad and Ramona Bass, co-executors of the estate of Langston Hughes.

Chronology

1902 James Langston Hughes is born February 1 in Joplin, Missouri, to James Nathaniel Hughes, a stenographer for a mining company, and Carrie Mercer Langston Hughes, a former government clerk.

1903 After his father immigrates to Mexico, Langston's mother takes him to Lawrence, Kansas, the home of Mary Langston, her twice-widowed mother. Mary Langston's first husband, Lewis Sheridan Leary, died fighting alongside John Brown at Harpers Ferry. Her second, Hughes's grandfather, was Charles Langston, a former abolitionist, Republican politician, and businessman.

1907 After a failed attempt at a reconciliation in Mexico, Langston and his mother return to Lawrence.

1909 Langston starts school in Topeka, Kansas, where he lives for a while with his mother before returning to his grandmother's home in Lawrence.

1915 Following Mary Langston's death, Hughes leaves Lawrence for Lincoln, Illinois, where his mother lives with her second husband, Homer Clark, and Homer Clark's young son by another union, Gwyn "Kit" Clark.

1916 Langston, elected class poet, graduates from the eighth grade. Moves to Cleveland, Ohio, and starts at Central High School there.

1918 Publishes early poems and short stories in his school's monthly magazine.

1919 Spends the summer in Toluca, Mexico, with his father.

1920 Graduates from Central High as class poet and editor of the school annual. Returns to Mexico to live with his father.

1921 In June, Hughes publishes "The Negro Speaks of Rivers" in *Crisis* magazine. In September, sponsored by his father, he enrolls at Columbia University in New York. Meets W. E. B. Du Bois, Jessie Fauset, and Countee Cullen.

1922   Unhappy at Columbia, Hughes withdraws from school and breaks with his father.

1923   Sailing in June to western Africa on the crew of a freighter, he visits Senegal, the Gold Coast, Nigeria, the Congo, and other countries.

1924   Spends several months in Paris working in the kitchen of a nightclub.

1925   Lives in Washington for a year with his mother. His poem "The Weary Blues" wins first prize in a contest sponsored by *Opportunity* magazine, which leads to a book contract with Knopf through Carl Van Vechten. Becomes friends with several other young artists of the Harlem Renaissance, including Zora Neale Hurston, Wallace Thurman, and Arna Bontemps.

1926   In January his first book, *The Weary Blues,* appears. He enrolls at historically black Lincoln University, Pennsylvania. In June, the *Nation* weekly magazine publishes his landmark essay "The Negro Artist and the Racial Mountain."

1927   Knopf publishes his second book of verse, *Fine Clothes to the Jew,* which is condemned in the black press. Hughes meets his powerful patron Mrs. Charlotte Osgood Mason. Travels in the South with Hurston, who is also taken up by Mrs. Mason.

1929   Hughes graduates from Lincoln University.

1930   Publishes his first novel, *Not without Laughter* (Knopf). Visits Cuba and meets fellow poet Nicolás Guillén. Hughes is dismissed by Mrs. Mason in a painful break made worse by false charges of dishonesty leveled by Hurston over their play *Mule Bone.*

1931   Demoralized, he travels to Haiti. Publishes work in the communist magazine *New Masses.* Supported by the Rosenwald Foundation, he tours the South taking his poetry to the people. In Alabama, he visits some of the Scottsboro Boys in prison. His brief collection of poems *Dear Lovely Death* is privately printed in Amenia, New York. Hughes and the illustrator Prentiss Taylor publish a verse pamphlet, *The Negro Mother.*

1932   With Taylor, he publishes *Scottsboro Limited,* a short play and four poems. From Knopf comes *The Dream Keeper,* a book of previously published poems selected for young people. Later, Macmillan brings out *Popo and Fifina,* a children's story about Haiti written with Arna Bontemps, his closest friend. In June, Hughes sails to Russia in a band of twenty-two young African Americans to make a film about race relations in the United States. After the project collapses, he lives for a year in the Soviet Union. Publishes his most radical verse, including "Good Morning Revolution" and "Goodbye Christ."

1933   Returns home at midyear via China and Japan. Supported by a patron, Noël Sullivan of San Francisco, Hughes spends a year in Carmel writing short stories.

1934   Knopf publishes his first short story collection, *The Ways of White Folks.* After labor unrest in California threatens his safety, he leaves for Mexico following news of his father's death.

1935   Spends several months in Mexico, mainly translating short stories by local leftist writers. Lives for some time with the photographer Henri Cartier-Bresson. Returning almost destitute to the United States, he joins his mother in Oberlin, Ohio. Visits New York for the Broadway production of his play *Mulatto* and clashes with its producer over changes in the script. Unhappy, he writes the poem "Let America Be America Again."

1936   Wins a Guggenheim Foundation fellowship for work on a novel but soon turns mainly to writing plays in association with the Karamu Theater in Cleveland. Karamu stages his farce *Little Ham* and his historical drama about Haiti, *Troubled Island.*

1937   Karamu stages *Joy to My Soul,* another comedy. In July, he visits Paris for the League of American Writers. He then travels to Spain, where he spends the rest of the year reporting on the civil war for the *Baltimore Afro-American.*

1938   In New York, Hughes founds the radical Harlem Suitcase Theater, which stages his agitprop play *Don't You Want to Be Free?* The leftist International Workers Order publishes *A New Song,* a pamphlet of radical verse. Karamu stages his play *Front Porch.* His mother dies.

1939   In Hollywood he writes the script for the movie *Way Down South*, which is criticized for stereotyping black life. Hughes goes for an extended stay in Carmel, California, again as the guest of Noël Sullivan.

1940   His autobiography *The Big Sea* appears (Knopf). He is picketed by a religious group for his poem "Goodbye Christ," which he publicly renounces.

1941   With a Rosenwald Fund fellowship for playwriting, he leaves California for Chicago, where he founds the Skyloft Players. Moves on to New York in December.

1942   Knopf publishes his book of verse *Shakespeare in Harlem*. The Skyloft Players stage his play *The Sun Do Move*. In the summer he resides at the Yaddo writers' and artists' colony, New York. Hughes also works as a writer in support of the war effort. In November he starts "Here to Yonder," a weekly column in the Chicago *Defender* newspaper.

1943   "Here to Yonder" introduces Jesse B. Semple, or Simple, a comic Harlem character who quickly becomes its most popular feature. Hughes publishes *Jim Crow's Last Stand* (Negro Publication Society of America), a pamphlet of verse about the struggle for civil rights.

1944   Comes under surveillance by the FBI because of his former radicalism.

1945   With Mercer Cook, translates and later publishes *Masters of the Dew* (Reynal and Hitchcock), a novel by Jacques Roumain of Haiti.

1947   His work as librettist with Kurt Weill and Elmer Rice on the Broadway musical play *Street Scene* brings Hughes a financial windfall. He vacations in Jamaica. Knopf publishes *Fields of Wonder*, his only book composed mainly of lyric poems on nonracial topics.

1948   Hughes is denounced (erroneously) as a communist in the U.S. Senate. He buys a townhouse in Harlem and moves in with his longtime friends Toy and Emerson Harper.

1949 Doubleday publishes *Poetry of the Negro, 1746–1949,* an anthology edited with Arna Bontemps. Also published are *One-Way Ticket* (Knopf), a book of poems, and *Cuba Libre: Poems of Nicolás Guillén* (Anderson and Ritchie), translated by Hughes and Ben Frederic Carruthers. Hughes teaches for three months at the University of Chicago Lab School for children. His opera about Haiti with William Grant Still, *Troubled Island,* is presented in New York.

1950 Another opera, *The Barrier,* with music by Jan Meyerowitz, is hailed in New York but later fails on Broadway. Simon and Schuster publishes *Simple Speaks His Mind,* the first of five books based on his newspaper columns.

1951 Hughes's book of poems about life in Harlem, *Montage of a Dream Deferred,* appears (Henry Holt).

1952 His second collection of short stories, *Laughing to Keep from Crying,* is published by Henry Holt. In its "First Book" series for children, Franklin Watts publishes Hughes's *The First Book of Negroes.*

1953 In March, forced to testify before Senator Joseph McCarthy's subcommittee on subversive activities, Hughes is exonerated after repudiating his past radicalism. *Simple Takes a Wife* appears.

1954 Mainly for young readers, he publishes *Famous Negro Americans* (Dodd, Mead) and *The First Book of Rhythms.*

1955 Publishes *The First Book of Jazz* and finishes *Famous Negro Music Makers* (Dodd, Mead). In November, Simon and Schuster publishes *The Sweet Flypaper of Life,* a narrative of Harlem with photographs by Roy DeCarava.

1956 Hughes's second volume of autobiography, *I Wonder As I Wander* (Rinehart), appears, as well as *A Pictorial History of the Negro* (Crown), coedited with Milton Meltzer, and *The First Book of the West Indies.*

1957 *Esther,* an opera with composer Jan Meyerowitz, has its premiere in Illinois. Rinehart publishes *Simple Stakes a Claim* as a novel. Hughes's musical play *Simply Heavenly,* based on his Simple character, runs for several weeks off and then on Broadway. Hughes translates and publishes *Selected Poems of Gabriela Mistral* (Indiana University Press).

1958 *The Langston Hughes Reader* (George Braziller) also appears, as well as *The Book of Negro Folklore* (Dodd, Mead), coedited with Arna Bontemps, and another juvenile, *Famous Negro Heroes of America* (Dodd, Mead). John Day publishes a short novel, *Tambourines to Glory,* based on a Hughes gospel musical play.

1959 Hughes's *Selected Poems* published (Knopf).

1960 *The First Book of Africa* appears, along with *An African Treasury: Articles, Essays, Stories, Poems by Black Africans,* edited by Hughes (Crown).

1961 Inducted into the National Institute of Arts and Letters. Knopf publishes his book-length poem *Ask Your Mama: 12 Moods for Jazz. The Best of Simple,* drawn from the columns, appears (Hill and Wang). Hughes writes his gospel musical plays *Black Nativity* and *The Prodigal Son.* He visits Africa again.

1962 Begins a weekly column for the *New York Post.* Attends a writers' conference in Uganda. Publishes *Fight for Freedom: The Story of the NAACP,* commissioned by the organization.

1963 His third collection of short stories, *Something in Common,* appears from Hill and Wang. Indiana University Press publishes *Five Plays by Langston Hughes,* edited by Webster Smalley, as well as Hughes's anthology *Poems from Black Africa, Ethiopia, and Other Countries.*

1964 His musical play *Jericho–Jim Crow,* a tribute to the civil rights movement, is staged in Greenwich Village. Indiana University Press brings out his anthology *New Negro Poets: U.S.A.,* with a foreword by Gwendolyn Brooks.

1965 With novelists Paule Marshall and William Melvin Kelley, Hughes visits Europe for the U.S. State Department. His gospel play *The Prodigal Son* and his cantata with music by David Amram, *Let Us Remember,* are staged.

1966 After twenty-three years, Hughes ends his depiction of Simple in his Chicago *Defender* column. Publishes *The Book of Negro*

Humor (Dodd, Mead). In a visit sponsored by the U.S. government, he is honored in Dakar, Senegal, at the First World Festival of Negro Arts.

1967   His *The Best Short Stories by Negro Writers: An Anthology from 1899 to the Present* (Little, Brown) includes the first published story by Alice Walker. On May 22, Hughes dies at New York Polyclinic Hospital in Manhattan from complications following prostate surgery. Later that year, two books appear: *The Panther and the Lash: Poems of Our Times* (Knopf) and, with Milton Meltzer, *Black Magic: A Pictorial History of the Negro in American Entertainment* (Prentice Hall).

The Collected Works of
Langston Hughes

Volume 1

The Poems: 1921–1940

Introduction

The poems in this volume represent the first generation of Langston Hughes's creativity as a writer, the years between 1921 and 1940. They take us as readers from the initial published articulation of his own distinct literary voice in 1921 to the era of his attainment of full poetic maturity by the end of the 1930s.

Exactly when Hughes wrote his first poem is not altogether clear. In his first book of autobiography, *The Big Sea* (1940), he tells of being elected by his fellow students (all but two of them white) as class poet in the eighth grade in Lincoln, Illinois, where he lived for a year. On graduation day, the applause of his listeners so delighted him when he recited the flattering poem he had composed about his teachers and the school that he committed himself there and then to a new interest: "That was the way I began to write poetry."[1]

This story may be apocryphal. We know that his mother, Carrie Mercer Langston Hughes, sometimes wrote verse, and also that from early in his childhood she and others had helped to give him a proper appreciation of the work of various classic writers, including the most admired African American poet at the turn of the century, Paul Laurence Dunbar. As a boy, Hughes loved books. He recalled discovering early, during what had been a lonely childhood, the unique consolations of literature. "Then it was," he declared, "that books began to happen to me, and I began to believe in nothing but books and the wonderful world in books— where if people suffered, they suffered in beautiful language, not in monosyllables, as we did in Kansas" (*TBS*, 16).

By his sophomore year in high school in Cleveland, Ohio, as the Central High School monthly magazine attests, Hughes was writing poetry fairly steadily and no doubt enjoying a growing reputation among his teachers and his fellow students as a budding author. In his adoles-

---

1. Langston Hughes, *The Big Sea* (New York: Alfred A. Knopf, 1940), 24 (hereafter cited as *TBS*).

cence, as might be expected, he was very much an imitative versifier captivated by conventional themes and jingling rhymes. He also wrote and published short stories. Indeed, Hughes credited a writer of fiction, Guy de Maupassant, rather than any poet, with his decision to become a serious writer. "I think it was de Maupassant," he recollected, "who made me really want to be a writer and write stories about Negroes, so true that people in far-away lands would read them—even after I was dead" (*TBS*, 34). Hughes would never give up writing fiction, or cease to take pride in his versatility in other literary forms, including essays and drama. However, at some point in his young manhood, he clearly began to see the composition of poetry as central to his identity as an author.

A major step came in high school around 1918 with his discovery of Walt Whitman, as may be seen in his awkward but unmistakably Whitmanesque poem "A Song of the Soul of Central." This paean in free verse (apparently the first free verse that Hughes wrote, and also the first published by anyone in the school magazine, according to an editorial note) saluted Central High for its democratic ideals and practices. The poem marks the beginning of his true appreciation of the challenge of exploring (as Whitman had done) the crucial relationship between American vernacular speech and traditional poetic practices, as well as between the nation's democratic ideals and the mysteries of poetic inspiration. From Whitman he gained a richer understanding of the dynamic role of democracy in the nation's life and art, as well as an eagerness to experiment with native forms in order to capture the peculiar genius of American and African American life. He learned much also from Whitman's disciple Carl Sandburg, who showed the way for the younger poet to become fascinated with jazz and other forms of popular music, and then to absorb such forms into his own literary practice. "I began to try to write like Carl Sandburg," he would recall (*TBS*, 28). And as Hughes achieved his first maturity, there was also the bracing example of the Jamaican-born poet Claude McKay. His two books *Spring in New Hampshire* (1920) and *Harlem Shadows* (1922) moved and instructed Hughes. McKay's place in progressive literary circles in New York as associate editor of *Liberator* magazine, along with his ability to maintain an artistic identity that allowed for both an intense lyricism and a passion for social and political issues, showed Hughes something of the range to which he might aspire as an African American thinker and writer coming of age in the 1920s.

By 1921, when he was nineteen, Hughes had found his own voice. Indeed, his first poem published in a national magazine, "The Negro Speaks of Rivers," which appeared that year in *Crisis,* the monthly magazine of the NAACP, became his signature poem, the one Hughes usually chose to conclude each of his many public readings. This poem shows the young poet employing for the first time rhythmic values emanating not from hoary poetic fashion but from his chosen subject— in this case, the spirituality and historicity of black culture. The poem came to him, Hughes claimed, on a train ride to Mexico to join his father, who lived there in prosperity. Because his money-conscious father seemed to hate not only art but also his fellow blacks ("My father hated Negroes. I think he hated himself, too, for being a Negro") Langston had begun to hate him and to dread the idea of living with him (*TBS,* 40). This intimate prompting did not, however, limit the range of "The Negro Speaks of Rivers." Rather than becoming overwhelmed by rage or fatalism, Hughes demonstrated what would be his characteristic ability as a poet to feel passionately and then to transcend raw emotion through a mastery of art that liberated him from excessive forms of invective or self-absorption.

In discussing the writing of "The Negro Speaks of Rivers," Hughes offered a glimpse of his general method of composition. A line had come to him ("I've known rivers") and then another ("I've known rivers ancient as the world . . . "). Soon the poem seemed to write itself. "No doubt," he concedes in *The Big Sea,* "I changed a few words the next day, or maybe crossed out a line or two. But there are seldom many changes in my poems, once they're down. Generally, the first two or three lines come to me from something I'm thinking about, or looking at, or doing, and the rest of the poem (if there is to be a poem) flows from those first few lines, usually right away. If there is a chance to put the poem down then, I write it down. If not, I try to remember it until I get to a pencil and paper; for poems are like rainbows: they escape you quickly" (*TBS,* 56).

Nevertheless, these words hardly constitute the full story of Hughes's aesthetic as a poet (any more than Robert Frost's remark about poems beginning as a lump in the throat does justice to the complexity of his art). Later in his career, Hughes often offered the notion that life makes poetry—that is, that he depended on situations he observed directly, or participated in, to inspire his verse. Accepting at one point a certain critic's description of Hughes as a documentary poet (whatever that term means), he did little to prevent the impression that an almost facile correspondence existed between his experiences and his verse. Perhaps not surprisingly, to some observers his poetry is far too simple to be admired. Hughes indeed wished to be understood clearly by his readers. On the whole, he had little time for, or patience with, those modernist poetic devices and approaches that tend to intimidate and alienate readers. He shunned the use of learned allusions, arcane vocabulary, and complicated syntax in favor of persistent clarity. In many ways, simplicity was the essence of his aesthetic. However, the sensitive reader soon discovers that in Hughes's art, as in so much of life, simplicity can be a complex affair.

From the start, his poetry flowed in certain fairly distinct streams. One is tempted to see as perhaps the most intimate stream those poems composed in his "lyric" mode, having little to do, at least on the surface, with social, historical, and political issues, or with overt references to African American culture. Certainly in the 1920s, when he established his reputation as a poet, and then again after 1940 or so, when he turned dramatically away from radical socialism, Hughes wrote many moving poems about nature. However, his vision of the natural world is hardly conventional. Nature in Hughes's verse can be emotional and spiritual therapy but also a chilling repository of what we might call existential gloom, as in "Winter Moon" ("How thin and sharp is the moon tonight! / How thin and sharp and ghostly white / Is the slim curved crook of the moon tonight!") A measure of despair was lodged deep in Hughes's consciousness, planted or encouraged there by the extreme loneliness of his childhood. In his poetry, as a result, the beauty of nature is seldom divorced from its more sinister and menacing aspects, its cold indifference to human life. In this general category one would have to place the remarkable number of Hughes's poems, incongruous in a writer so strongly associated with joy and laughter, that deal with suicide and death ("Dear Lovely Death," as he entitled one poem).

Another, no doubt more recognizable stream in Hughes's poetry is that comprising poems that protest, directly or indirectly, against social injustice. "The Negro Speaks of Rivers" exemplifies the power of indirection; but early poems such as "The South" ("The lazy, laughing South / With blood on its mouth") or "The White Ones" ("I do not hate you, / For your faces are beautiful, too") look straight into the hard face of racism and speak truth to white power. From the start, too, Hughes used his pen to inveigh against poverty as it affects people across racial lines, as in "Grant Park" ("The haunting face of poverty, / The hands of pain"); or to inveigh against colonialism and imperialism, as in "Johannesburg Mines" ("In the Johannesburg mines / There are 240,000 / Native Africans working"). All his life, so it often seems, Hughes wrote mainly in order to protest. He took seriously the tradition of political resistance to tyranny or injustice into which he had been born. This tradition reached far back into his family's history—indeed, past segregation, the Civil War, and slavery at least to the war of American independence and the white Virginia planter who had been his maternal great-grandfather. Hughes's sense of social injustice was not limited by race. After all, the abolitionist movement in which his grandparents had served certainly had asserted the human dignity of black slaves; and Hughes's high school, dominated by the children of immigrants from eastern Europe (many of Hughes's classmates openly celebrated the Russian Revolution of 1917), seemed to him to capture an ideal vision of interracial solidarity.

In the 1930s, this political aspect of Hughes's poetry reached its zenith. Driven by a number of factors, including an emotional crisis caused by his rejection by an important patron, as well as by the economic depression that had settled gloomily over American society, Hughes embraced radical socialism with a vengeance (although he never became a party member). As a poet he turned away from the inspiration of the blues and jazz, as well as from writing lyric verse and other forms that now seemed politically regressive. In their place came hortatory poems such as

"Good Morning Revolution" and "Goodbye Christ," "One More 'S' in the U.S.A." ("To make it Soviet") and "Revolution" ("Great mob that knows no fear— / Come here!"). In this radical sphere Hughes now and then could also strike mellower notes, as in his haunting "Let America Be American Again," written in 1935 as an anthem for a struggling nation.

Around 1940, hounded by an evangelical group because of his jeering reference to its leader in the poem "Goodbye Christ," but spurred also by patriotic considerations as the world war approached America, Hughes ceased writing radical socialist verse and specifically repudiated that poem. His autobiography *The Big Sea,* published that year, barely mentions his former interest in radical politics. However, even in the heyday of his radicalism, Hughes never lost sight of the special plight of African Americans and delighted in being hailed by blacks as virtually the poet laureate of the race. In his landmark essay "The Negro Artist and the Racial Mountain," published in June 1926 in the *Nation* weekly magazine and almost immediately recognized as a major manifesto of the Harlem Renaissance, Hughes began by asserting his disdain for a certain young black writer who wanted to be seen as a poet but not a Negro poet. "No great poet," Hughes declared, "has ever been afraid of being himself." He deplored "this urge within the race toward white-ness, the desire to pour racial individuality into the mold of American standardization, and to be as little Negro and as much American as possible."[2] Nevertheless, the essay emphasizes at its end the right of younger black artists to compose exactly as they themselves wished no matter what blacks or whites thought. Accordingly, Hughes wrote poetry that honored elements of black culture historically denied by most whites and middle-class blacks. The speaker of the "Proem" to *The Weary Blues* asserts without regret or ambivalence, "I am a Negro: / Black as the night is black, / Black like the depths of my Africa." Whatever the cultural losses and erasures of slavery, Hughes believed, black Americans had a genuine history, a past that went far beyond American servitude back into Africa—and even a past within American slavery of which they should be proud.

2. "The Negro Artist and the Racial Mountain," *Nation* 122 (June 23, 1926): 692.

As a poet Hughes repudiated class privilege and embraced the poorest blacks as his true brothers and sisters. They were (in "Laughers") "Dream singers, / Story tellers, / Dancers, / Loud laughers in the hands of Fate— / My people." In a world that worshiped white beauty above all, this poet assured blacks of their own loveliness, and of the loveliness of their souls, as in "Poem":

> The night is beautiful,
> So the faces of my people.
>
> The stars are beautiful,
> So the eyes of my people.
>
> Beautiful, also, is the sun.
> Beautiful, also, are the souls of my people.

Such poems were a revelation to the many black Americans who historically had been taught to regard themselves as ugly and as representative of the more degraded side of nature. Other poets before Hughes, including Dunbar and James Weldon Johnson, had sung the merits of this or that aspect of black culture. Hughes, however, looked directly into the faces and hearts of black men and women and sought to assure them of the beauty of their bodies and their souls. Such poems eventually made him, among black Americans, the most beloved and revered of poets.

Of the most profound consequence to Hughes's art, however, was not simply his bold assertions of black beauty, historicity, and spirituality but the multiple ways in which this love of African American culture formally shaped his work. In this crucial matter of artistic influence, he saw the black masses as his indispensable tutors and guides. In 1925, even as he was preparing his first book of verse, he quietly took instruction from blacks living in the Seventh Street slum district near the capitol in Washington, D.C. "I tried to write poems," he declared, "like the songs they sang on Seventh Street—gay songs, because you had to be gay or die; sad songs, because you couldn't help being sad sometimes. But gay or sad, you kept on living and you kept on going. Their songs—the songs of Seventh Street—had the pulse beat of the people who keep on going."

The one reliable metronome of blacks' racial grace, Hughes believed, was their music. Whatever distinction his poetry possesses surely owes more to his regard for black music than to any other source. "Like the waves of the sea coming one after another," he wrote in tribute, "always one after another, like the earth moving around the sun, night, day—night, day—night, day—forever, so is the undertow of black music with its rhythm that never betrays you, its strength like the beat of the human heart, its humor and its rooted power" (*TBS,* 209).

Plunging into African American culture meant sooner or later confronting questions about the use of dialect, a controversial aspect of black writing since the late nineteenth century. As a poet, Paul Laurence Dunbar had taken black dialect to the heights of technical proficiency as well as popularity; but even in his skilled hands black dialect could not shake off its demeaning associations with stereotypes of the comic "darky," of insulting minstrelsy, and of ignorance as the inevitable condition of black culture. In 1922, in his important anthology *The Book of American Negro Poetry,* James Weldon Johnson declared black dialect dead as a factor in verse, unacceptable in the modern age. Yet even then, in poems such as the beloved "Mother to Son" ("Life for me ain't been no crystal stair") and "Song for a Banjo Dance" ("Shake your brown feet, honey, / Shake your brown feet, chile"), Hughes was breathing new life into the poetic usage of black vernacular speech. Then, when he became entranced by the blues and made it central to his volume *Fine Clothes to the Jew* (1927), he did at least as much as anyone to return dignity and emotional depth to the uses of black dialect in American literature.

Some of his earliest poems, such as "Danse Africaine," showed Hughes interested in what we now see as stereotypes of black exoticism ("The low beating of the tom-toms, / The slow beating of the tom-toms, / Low . . . slow, / Slow . . . low, / Stirs your blood"). Soon, however, as in "Negro Dancers," he was imaginatively exploring black music and dance as one might find it in Harlem cabarets: "Me an' ma baby's / Got two mo' ways, / Two mo' ways to do de buck!" The next important step was his growing immersion in jazz, especially when he spent several months in Paris working in the kitchen of a nightclub featuring jazz performers from back home. "Jazz Band in a Parisian Cabaret" begins:

Play that thing,
Jazz band!
Play it for the lords and ladies,
For the dukes and counts,
For the whores and gigolos,
For the American millionaires,
And the school teachers
Out for a spree.
Play it,
Jazz band!

And then jazz began to meld in Hughes's work with what would be the prime musical inspiration of his life—the music called the blues. These songs of love and loss, laced with often mordant humor, seemed to him to capture more precisely than any other form the essence of the peculiar African American response to the pain and pleasure of life. His poem "The Weary Blues" (the first he had written that honored the blues) gave him the title for his first book; but the blues so saturated the text of his second, *Fine Clothes to the Jew,* that it elicited mainly howls of protest in the black press. Critics were appalled that Hughes would take such topics as sex and violence among the "lowest" blacks as fitting subjects for poetry. This volume, included in its entirety here, was Hughes's poorest selling but perhaps most important single work, a breakthrough in black literary culture on a par, in its own way, with the effect of Whitman's "scandalous" *Leaves of Grass* of 1855.

Hughes survived such criticism by dint of his unbreakable confidence in himself and his art, as well as his unbreakable confidence in the people who mattered most to him. Throughout his life he never ceased to write poetry, even when its financial rewards were negligible and his own financial situation was precarious at best. Despite his seemingly casual approach to art as well as life, he was sustained throughout by a deep regard for the prophetic role of the poet and the light that poetry uniquely sheds on the human condition. "What is poetry?" he asked rhetorically near the end of his life. "It is the human soul entire," he answered, "squeezed like a lemon or lime, into atomic words." How should a poet relate to his or her cultural and political situation? A poet was a human being, Hughes insisted on pointing out, and "each human being must live within his time, with and for his people, and within the boundaries of his country." Above all, a poet must possess courage, and dare to speak truth. There could be no salvation in unseemly compromise, nor any ultimate relief in timidity. "Hang yourself, poet, in your own words," Hughes urged. "Otherwise, you are dead."[3]

3. Langston Hughes, "Draft Ideas," December 3, 1964. Langston Hughes Papers, James Weldon Johnson Memorial Collection, Beinecke Rare Book and Manuscript Library, Yale University. Quoted more extensively in Arnold Rampersad, *The Life of Langston Hughes, Volume II: I Dream a World* (New York: Oxford University Press, 1988), 85.

A Note on the Text

In presenting this three-volume edition of the poems of Langston Hughes as part of our *Collected Works of Langston Hughes,* we have chosen to highlight the individual books of verse prepared and published by Hughes, as opposed to a presentation of each poem in strict chronological order according to the date of its first publication, as in *The Collected Poems of Langston Hughes,* edited by Arnold Rampersad and David Roessel (New York: Knopf, 1994).

Thus, in Volume 1 (1921–1940) we offer the texts of four complete books of poems—*The Weary Blues* (1926), *Fine Clothes to the Jew* (1927), *Dear Lovely Death* (1931), and *A New Song* (1938). We exclude *The Dream Keeper* (1932) because this collection, intended for younger readers, reprints poems from Hughes's previous volumes of verse.

"Uncollected" poems from 1921 to 1940, if they did not appear in a later book of verse prepared by Hughes, are presented in chronological order according to the date of their first publication. The texts of these "uncollected" poems come in general from Rampersad and Roessel, eds., *Collected Poems of Langston Hughes.* This volume, which presents the *last* published version of each poem, should be consulted for its bibliographical notes and other information.

The Weary Blues

(1926)

To my mother

I wish to thank the editors of *The Crisis, Opportunity, Survey Graphic, Vanity Fair, The World Tomorrow* and *The Amsterdam News* for having first published some of the poems in this book.

Contents

Proem

I am a Negro:
    Black as the night is black,
    Black like the depths of my Africa.

I've been a slave:
    Cæsar told me to keep his door-steps clean.
    I brushed the boots of Washington.

I've been a worker:
    Under my hand the pyramids arose.
    I made mortar for the Woolworth Building.

I've been a singer:
    All the way from Africa to Georgia
    I carried my sorrow songs.
    I made ragtime.

I've been a victim:
    The Belgians cut off my hands in the Congo.
    They lynch me now in Texas.

I am a Negro:
    Black as the night is black,
    Black like the depths of my Africa.

The Weary Blues

The Weary Blues *imitates the music*

1 Droning a drowsy syncopated tune,
Rocking back and forth to a mellow croon,
    I heard a Negro play.
Down on Lenox Avenue the other night
5 By the pale dull pallor of an old gas light
        He did a lazy sway. . . . *repition creates a drag to it*
        He did a lazy sway. . . . *"weary"*
To the tune o' those Weary Blues.
With his ebony hands on each ivory key
10 He made that poor piano moan with melody. *alliteration*
        O Blues! ← *mournful*
Swaying to and fro on his rickety stool
He played that sad raggy tune like a musical fool.
        Sweet Blues!
15 Coming from a black man's soul.
        O Blues!
In a deep song voice with a melancholy tone
I heard that Negro sing, that old piano moan—
        "Ain't got nobody in all this world,
20 Ain't got nobody but ma self.
        I's gwine to quit ma frownin'
        And put ma troubles on the shelf."
Thump, thump, thump, went his foot on the floor.
He played a few chords then he sang some more—
25 "I got the Weary Blues
    And I can't be satisfied.
    Got the Weary Blues
    And can't be satisfied—
    I ain't happy no mo'

30   And I wish that I had died."
And far into the night he crooned that tune.
The stars went out and so did the moon.
The singer stopped playing and went to bed
While the Weary Blues echoed through his head.
35 He slept like a rock or a man that's dead.

Jazzonia

Oh, silver tree!
Oh, shining rivers of the soul!

In a Harlem cabaret
Six long-headed jazzers play.
A dancing girl whose eyes are bold
Lifts high a dress of silken gold.

Oh, singing tree!
Oh, shining rivers of the soul!

Were Eve's eyes
In the first garden
Just a bit too bold?
Was Cleopatra gorgeous
In a gown of gold?

Oh, shining tree!
Oh, silver rivers of the soul!

In a whirling cabaret
Six long-headed jazzers play.

Negro Dancers

"Me an' ma baby's
Got two mo' ways,
Two mo' ways to do de buck!
　Da, da,
　Da, da, da!
Two mo' ways to do de buck!"

Soft light on the tables,
Music gay,
Brown-skin steppers
In a cabaret.

White folks, laugh!
White folks, pray!

"Me an' ma baby's
Got two mo' ways,
Two mo' ways to do de buck!"

The Cat and the Saxophone
(2 A.M.)

EVERYBODY
Half-pint,—
Gin?
No, make it
LOVES MY BABY
corn. You like
liquor,
don't you, honey?
BUT MY BABY
Sure. Kiss me,

DON'T LOVE NOBODY
daddy.
BUT ME.
Say!
EVERYBODY
Yes?
WANTS MY BABY
I'm your
BUT MY BABY
sweetie, ain't I?
DON'T WANT NOBODY
Sure.
BUT
Then let's
ME,
do it!
SWEET ME.
Charleston,
mamma!
!

Young Singer

One who sings "chansons vulgaires"
In a Harlem cellar
Where the jazz-band plays
From dark to dawn
Would not understand
Should you tell her
That she is like a nymph
For some wild faun.

Cabaret

Does a jazz-band ever sob?
They say a jazz-band's gay.
Yet as the vulgar dancers whirled
And the wan night wore away,
One said she heard the jazz-band sob
When the little dawn was grey.

To Midnight Nan at Leroy's

Strut and wiggle,
Shameless gal.
Wouldn't no good fellow
Be your pal.

Hear dat music. . . .
Jungle night.
Hear dat music. . . .
And the moon was white.

Sing your Blues song,
Pretty baby.
You want lovin'
And you don't mean maybe.

Jungle lover. . . .
Night black boy. . . .
Two against the moon
And the moon was joy.

Strut and wiggle,
Shameless Nan.
Wouldn't no good fellow
Be your man.

To a Little Lover-Lass, Dead

She
Who searched for lovers
In the night
Has gone the quiet way
Into the still,
Dark land of death
Beyond the rim of day.

Now like a little lonely waif
She walks
An endless street
And gives her kiss to nothingness.
Would God his lips were sweet!

Harlem Night Club

Sleek black boys in a cabaret.
Jazz-band, jazz-band,—
Play, plAY, PLAY!
Tomorrow. . . . who knows?
Dance today!

White girls' eyes
Call gay black boys.
Black boys' lips
Grin jungle joys.

Dark brown girls
In blond men's arms.
Jazz-band, jazz-band,—
Sing Eve's charms!

imitate a fast tempo music, quickness of a night club

White ones, brown ones,
What do you know
About tomorrow
Where all paths go?

Jazz-boys, jazz-boys,—
Play, plAY, PLAY!
Tomorrow. . . . is darkness.
Joy today!

Nude Young Dancer

What jungle tree have you slept under,
Midnight dancer of the jazzy hour?
What great forest has hung its perfume
Like a sweet veil about your bower?

What jungle tree have you slept under,
Night-dark girl of the swaying hips?
What star-white moon has been your mother?
To what clean boy have you offered your lips?

Young Prostitute

[handwritten: irony]

Her dark brown face
Is like a withered flower *[handwritten: implies she's old, but she's young]*
On a broken stem.
Those kind come cheap in Harlem
So they say.

[handwritten: irony as there's a tremendous price on the girl]

To a Black Dancer in "The Little Savoy"

Wine-maiden
Of the jazz-tuned night,
Lips
Sweet as purple dew,
Breasts
Like the pillows of all sweet dreams,
Who crushed
The grapes of joy
And dripped their juice
On you?

Song for a Banjo Dance

Shake your brown feet, honey,
Shake your brown feet, chile,
Shake your brown feet, honey,
Shake 'em swift and wil'—
   Get way back, honey,
   Do that low-down step.
   Walk on over, darling,
     Now! Come out
     With your left.
Shake your brown feet, honey,
Shake 'em, honey chile.

Sun's going down this evening—
Might never rise no mo'.
The sun's going down this very night—
Might never rise no mo'—
So dance with swift feet, honey,
   (The banjo's sobbing low)

Dance with swift feet, honey—
   Might never dance no mo'.

Shake your brown feet, Liza,
Shake 'em, Liza, chile,
Shake your brown feet, Liza,
   (The music's soft and wil')
Shake your brown feet, Liza,
   (The banjo's sobbing low)
The sun's going down this very night—
   Might never rise no mo'.

Blues Fantasy

Hey! Hey!
That's what the
Blues singers say.
Singing minor melodies
They laugh,
Hey! Hey!

My man's done left me,
Chile, he's gone away.
My good man's left me,
Babe, he's gone away.
Now the cryin' blues
Haunts me night and day.

Hey! . . . Hey!

Weary,
Weary,
Trouble, pain.
Sun's gonna shine

Somewhere
Again.

I got a railroad ticket,
Pack my trunk and ride.

Sing 'em, sister!

Got a railroad ticket,
Pack my trunk and ride.
And when I get on the train
I'll cast my blues aside.

Laughing,
Hey! . . . Hey!
Laugh a loud,
Hey! Hey!

Lenox Avenue: Midnight

The rhythm of life
Is a jazz rhythm,
Honey.
The gods are laughing at us.

The broken heart of love,
The weary, weary heart of pain,—
    Overtones,
    Undertones,
To the rumble of street cars,
To the swish of rain.

Lenox Avenue,
Honey.
Midnight,
And the gods are laughing at us.

Dream Variations

Dream Variation

To fling my arms wide
In some place of the sun,
To whirl and to dance
Till the white day is done.
Then rest at cool evening
Beneath a tall tree
While night comes on gently,
   Dark like me,—
That is my dream!

To fling my arms wide
In the face of the sun,
Dance! whirl! whirl!
Till the quick day is done.
Rest at pale evening. . . .
A tall, slim tree. . . .
Night coming tenderly
   Black like me.

Winter Moon

How thin and sharp is the moon tonight!
How thin and sharp and ghostly white
Is the slim curved crook of the moon tonight!

Poème d'Automne

The autumn leaves
Are too heavy with color.
The slender trees
On the Vulcan Road
Are dressed in scarlet and gold
Like young courtesans
Waiting for their lovers.
But soon
The winter winds
Will strip their bodies bare
And then
The sharp, sleet-stung
Caresses of the cold
Will be their only
Love.

Fantasy in Purple

Beat the drums of tragedy for me.
Beat the drums of tragedy and death.
And let the choir sing a stormy song
To drown the rattle of my dying breath.

Beat the drums of tragedy for me,
And let the white violins whir thin and slow,
But blow one blaring trumpet note of sun
To go with me
                    to the darkness
                              where I go.

March Moon

The moon is naked.
The wind has undressed the moon.
The wind has blown all the cloud-garments
Off the body of the moon
And now she's naked,
Stark naked.

But why don't you blush,
O shameless moon?
Don't you know
It isn't nice to be naked?

Joy

I went to look for Joy,
Slim, dancing Joy,
Gay, laughing Joy,
Bright-eyed Joy,—
And I found her
Driving the butcher's cart
In the arms of the butcher boy!
Such company, such company,
As keeps this young nymph, Joy!

The Negro Speaks of Rivers

The Negro Speaks of Rivers

(To W. E. B. DuBois)

I've known rivers:
I've known rivers ancient as the world and older than the
  flow of human blood in human veins.

My soul has grown deep like the rivers.

I bathed in the Euphrates when dawns were young.
I built my hut near the Congo and it lulled me to sleep.
I looked upon the Nile and raised the pyramids above it.
I heard the singing of the Mississippi when Abe Lincoln
  went down to New Orleans, and I've seen its muddy
  bosom turn all golden in the sunset.

I've known rivers:
Ancient, dusky rivers.

My soul has grown deep like the rivers.

Cross

My old man's a white old man
And my old mother's black.
If ever I cursed my white old man
I take my curses back.

If ever I cursed my black old mother
And wished she were in hell,
I'm sorry for that evil wish
And now I wish her well.

My old man died in a fine big house.
My ma died in a shack.
I wonder where I'm gonna die,
Being neither white nor black?

The Jester

In one hand
I hold tragedy
And in the other
Comedy,—
Masks for the soul.
Laugh with me.
You would laugh!
Weep with me.
You would weep!
Tears are my laughter.
Laughter is my pain.
Cry at my grinning mouth,
If you will.
Laugh at my sorrow's reign.
I am the Black Jester,
The dumb clown of the world,
The booted, booted fool of silly men.
Once I was wise.
Shall I be wise again?

The South

The lazy, laughing South
With blood on its mouth.
The sunny-faced South,
    Beast-strong,

Idiot-brained.
The child-minded South
Scratching in the dead fire's ashes
For a Negro's bones.
   Cotton and the moon,
   Warmth, earth, warmth,
   The sky, the sun, the stars,
   The magnolia-scented South.
Beautiful, like a woman,
Seductive as a dark-eyed whore,
   Passionate, cruel,
   Honey-lipped, syphilitic—
   That is the South.
And I, who am black, would love her
But she spits in my face.
And I, who am black,
Would give her many rare gifts
But she turns her back upon me.
   So now I seek the North—
   The cold-faced North,
   For she, they say,
   Is a kinder mistress,
And in her house my children
May escape the spell of the South.

As I Grew Older

It was a long time ago.
I have almost forgotten my dream.
But it was there then,
In front of me,
Bright like a sun,—
My dream.

And then the wall rose,
Rose slowly,
Slowly,
Between me and my dream.
Rose slowly, slowly,
Dimming,
Hiding,
The light of my dream.
Rose until it touched the sky,—
The wall.

Shadow.
I am black.

I lie down in the shadow.
No longer the light of my dream before me,
Above me.
Only the thick wall.
Only the shadow.

My hands!
My dark hands!
Break through the wall!
Find my dream!
Help me to shatter this darkness,
To smash this night,
To break this shadow
Into a thousand lights of sun,
Into a thousand whirling dreams
Of sun!

Aunt Sue's Stories

Aunt Sue has a head full of stories.
Aunt Sue has a whole heart full of stories.
Summer nights on the front porch
Aunt Sue cuddles a brown-faced child to her bosom
And tells him stories.

Black slaves
Working in the hot sun,
And black slaves
Walking in the dewy night,
And black slaves
Singing sorrow songs on the banks of a mighty river
Mingle themselves softly
In the flow of old Aunt Sue's voice,
Mingle themselves softly
In the dark shadows that cross and recross
Aunt Sue's stories.

And the dark-faced child, listening,
Knows that Aunt Sue's stories are real stories.
He knows that Aunt Sue
Never got her stories out of any book at all,
But that they came
Right out of her own life.

And the dark-faced child is quiet
Of a summer night
Listening to Aunt Sue's stories.

Poem

The night is beautiful,
So the faces of my people.

The stars are beautiful,
So the eyes of my people.

Beautiful, also, is the sun.
Beautiful, also, are the souls of my people.

A Black Pierrot

A Black Pierrot

I am a black Pierrot:
   She did not love me,
   So I crept away into the night
   And the night was black, too.

I am a black Pierrot:
   She did not love me,
   So I wept until the red dawn
   Dripped blood over the eastern hills
   And my heart was bleeding, too.

I am a black Pierrot:
   She did not love me,
   So with my once gay-colored soul
   Shrunken like a balloon without air,
   I went forth in the morning
   To seek a new brown love.

Harlem Night Song

Come,
Let us roam the night together
Singing.

I love you.

Across
The Harlem roof-tops
Moon is shining.

Night sky is blue.
Stars are great drops
Of golden dew.
In the cabaret
The jazz-band's playing.

I love you.

Come,
Let us roam the night together
Singing.

Songs to the Dark Virgin

I
Would
That I were a jewel,
A shattered jewel,
That all my shining brilliants
Might fall at thy feet,
Thou dark one.

II
Would
That I were a garment,
A shimmering, silken garment,
That all my folds
Might wrap about thy body,
Absorb thy body,
Hold and hide thy body,
Thou dark one.

III
Would
That I were a flame,

But one sharp, leaping flame
To annihilate thy body,
Thou dark one.

Ardella

I would liken you
To a night without stars
Were it not for your eyes.
I would liken you
To a sleep without dreams
Were it not for your songs.

Poem
To the Black Beloved

Ah,
My black one,
Thou art not beautiful
Yet thou hast
A loveliness
Surpassing beauty.

Oh,
My black one,
Thou art not good
Yet thou hast
A purity
Surpassing goodness.

Ah,
My black one,
Thou art not luminous

Yet an altar of jewels,
An altar of shimmering jewels,
Would pale in the light
Of thy darkness,
Pale in the light
Of thy nightness.

When Sue Wears Red

When Susanna Jones wears red
Her face is like an ancient cameo
Turned brown by the ages.

Come with a blast of trumpets,
    Jesus!

When Susanna Jones wears red
A queen from some time-dead Egyptian night
Walks once again.

Blow trumpets, Jesus!

And the beauty of Susanna Jones in red
Burns in my heart a love-fire sharp like pain.

Sweet silver trumpets,
    Jesus!

Pierrot

I work all day,
Said Simple John,
Myself a house to buy.
I work all day,

Said Simple John,
But Pierrot wondered why.

For Pierrot loved the long white road,
And Pierrot loved the moon,
And Pierrot loved a star-filled sky,
And the breath of a rose in June.

I have one wife,
Said Simple John,
And, faith, I love her yet.
I have one wife,
Said Simple John,
But Pierrot left Pierrette.

For Pierrot saw a world of girls,
And Pierrot loved each one,
And Pierrot thought all maidens fair
As flowers in the sun.

Oh, I am good,
Said Simple John,
The Lord will take me in.
Yes, I am good,
Said Simple John,
But Pierrot's steeped in sin.

For Pierrot played on a slim guitar,
And Pierrot loved the moon,
And Pierrot ran down the long white road
With the burgher's wife one June.

Water-Front Streets

Water-Front Streets

The spring is not so beautiful there,—
    But dream ships sail away
To where the spring is wondrous rare
    And life is gay.

The spring is not so beautiful there,—
    But lads put out to sea
Who carry beauties in their hearts
    And dreams, like me.

A Farewell

With gypsies and sailors,
Wanderers of the hills and seas,
I go to seek my fortune.
With pious folk and fair
I must have a parting.
But you will not miss me,—
You who live between the hills
And have never seen the seas.

Long Trip

The sea is a wilderness of waves,
A desert of water.
We dip and dive,
Rise and roll,

Hide and are hidden
On the sea.
   Day, night,
   Night, day,
The sea is a desert of waves,
A wilderness of water.

Port Town

Hello, sailor boy,
In from the sea!
Hello, sailor,
Come with me!

Come on drink cognac.
Rather have wine?
Come here, I love you.
Come and be mine.

Lights, sailor boy,
Warm, white lights.
Solid land, kid.
Wild, white nights.

Come on, sailor,
Out o' the sea.
Let's go, sweetie!
Come with me.

Sea Calm

How still,
How strangely still
The water is today.

It is not good
For water
To be so still that way.

Caribbean Sunset

God having a hemorrhage,
Blood coughed across the sky,
Staining the dark sea red,
That is sunset in the Caribbean.

Young Sailor

He carries
His own strength
And his own laughter,
His own today
And his own hereafter,—
This strong young sailor
Of the wide seas.

What is money for?
To spend, he says.
And wine?
To drink.
And women?
To love.
And today?
For joy.
And tomorrow?
For joy.
And the green sea
For strength,

And the brown land
For laughter.
And nothing hereafter.

Seascape

Off the coast of Ireland
   As our ship passed by
We saw a line of fishing ships
   Etched against the sky.

Off the coast of England
   As we rode the foam
We saw an Indian merchantman
   Coming home.

Natcha

Natcha, offering love.
For ten shillings offering love.
Offering: A night with me, honey.
A long, sweet night with me.
   Come, drink palm wine.
   Come, drink kisses.
A long, dream night with me.

Sea Charm

Sea charm
The sea's own children
Do not understand.
They know

But that the sea is strong
Like God's hand.
They know
But that sea wind is sweet
Like God's breath,
And that the sea holds
A wide, deep death.

Death of an Old Seaman

We buried him high on a windy hill,
But his soul went out to sea.
I know, for I heard, when all was still,
His sea-soul say to me:

Put no tombstone at my head,
For here I do not make my bed.
Strew no flowers on my grave,
I've gone back to the wind and wave.
Do not, do not weep for me,
For I am happy with my sea.

Shadows in the Sun

Beggar Boy

What is there within this beggar lad
That I can neither hear nor feel nor see,
That I can neither know nor understand
And still it calls to me?

Is not he but a shadow in the sun—
A bit of clay, brown, ugly, given life?
And yet he plays upon his flute a wild free tune
As if Fate had not bled him with her knife!

Troubled Woman

She stands
In the quiet darkness,
This troubled woman,
Bowed by
Weariness and pain,
Like an
Autumn flower
In the frozen rain.
Like a
Wind-blown autumn flower
That never lifts its head
Again.

Suicide's Note

The calm,
Cool face of the river
Asked me for a kiss.

Sick Room

How quiet
It is in this sick room
Where on the bed
A silent woman lies between two lovers—
Life and Death,
And all three covered with a sheet of pain.

Soledad
A Cuban Portrait

The shadows
Of too many nights of love
Have fallen beneath your eyes.
Your eyes,
So full of pain and passion,
So full of lies.
So full of pain and passion,
Soledad,
So deeply scarred,
So still with silent cries.

To the Dark Mercedes of "El Palacio de Amor"

Mercedes is a jungle-lily in a death house.
Mercedes is a doomed star.
Mercedes is a charnel rose.
Go where gold
Will fall at the feet of your beauty,
Mercedes.
Go where they will pay you well
For your loveliness.

Mexican Market Woman

This ancient hag
Who sits upon the ground
Selling her scanty wares
Day in, day round,
Has known high wind-swept mountains,
And the sun has made
Her skin so brown.

After Many Springs

Now,
In June,
When the night is a vast softness
Filled with blue stars,
And broken shafts of moon-glimmer
Fall upon the earth,
Am I too old to see the fairies dance?
I cannot find them any more.

Young Bride

They say she died,—
Although I do not know,
They say she died of grief
And in the earth-dark arms of Death
Sought calm relief,
And rest from pain of love
In loveless sleep.

The Dream Keeper

Bring me all of your dreams,
You dreamers.
Bring me all of your
Heart melodies
That I may wrap them
In a blue cloud-cloth
Away from the too rough fingers
Of the world.

Poem
(To F. S.)

I loved my friend.
He went away from me.
There's nothing more to say.
The poem ends,
Soft as it began,—
I loved my friend.

Our Land

Our Land
Poem for a Decorative Panel

We should have a land of sun,
Of gorgeous sun,
And a land of fragrant water
Where the twilight
Is a soft bandanna handkerchief
Of rose and gold,
And not this land where life is cold.

We should have a land of trees,
Of tall thick trees
Bowed down with chattering parrots
Brilliant as the day,
And not this land where birds are grey.

Ah, we should have a land of joy,
Of love and joy and wine and song,
And not this land where joy is wrong.

Oh, sweet, away!
Ah, my beloved one, away!

Lament for Dark Peoples

I was a red man one time,
But the white men came.
I was a black man, too,
But the white men came.

They drove me out of the forest.
They took me away from the jungles.
I lost my trees.
I lost my silver moons.

Now they've caged me
In the circus of civilization.
Now I herd with the many—
Caged in the circus of civilization.

Afraid

We cry among the skyscrapers
As our ancestors
Cried among the palms in Africa
Because we are alone,
It is night,
And we're afraid.

Poem

For the portrait of an African boy after the manner of Gauguin

All the tom-toms of the jungles beat in my blood,
And all the wild hot moons of the jungles shine in my soul.
I am afraid of this civilization—
        So hard,
            So strong,
                So cold.

Summer Night

The sounds
Of the Harlem night
Drop one by one into stillness.
The last player-piano is closed.
The last victrola ceases with the
"Jazz Boy Blues."
The last crying baby sleeps
And the night becomes
Still as a whispering heartbeat.
I toss
Without rest in the darkness,
Weary as the tired night,
My soul
Empty as the silence,
Empty with a vague,
Aching emptiness,
Desiring,
Needing someone,
Something.

I toss without rest
In the darkness
Until the new dawn,
Wan and pale,
Descends like a white mist
Into the court-yard.

Disillusion

I would be simple again,
Simple and clean
Like the earth,

Like the rain,
Nor ever know,
Dark Harlem,
The wild laughter
Of your mirth
Nor the salt tears
Of your pain.
Be kind to me,
Oh, great dark city.
Let me forget.
I will not come
To you again.

Danse Africaine

The low beating of the tom-toms,
The slow beating of the tom-toms,
   Low . . . slow
   Slow . . . low—
   Stirs your blood.
     Dance!
A night-veiled girl
   Whirls softly into a
   Circle of light.
   Whirls softly . . . slowly,
Like a wisp of smoke around the fire—
   And the tom-toms beat,
   And the tom-toms beat,
And the low beating of the tom-toms
   Stirs your blood.

The White Ones

I do not hate you,
For your faces are beautiful, too.
I do not hate you,
Your faces are whirling lights of loveliness and splendor, too.
Yet why do you torture me,
O, white strong ones,
Why do you torture me?

Mother to Son

Well, son, I'll tell you:
Life for me ain't been no crystal stair.
It's had tacks in it,
And splinters,
And boards torn up,
And places with no carpet on the floor—
Bare.
But all the time
I'se been a-climbin' on,
And reachin' landin's,
And turnin' corners,
And sometimes goin' in the dark
Where there ain't been no light.
So boy, don't you turn back.
Don't you set down on the steps
'Cause you finds it's kinder hard.
Don't you fall now—
For I'se still goin', honey,
I'se still climbin',
And life for me ain't been no crystal stair.

Poem

We have tomorrow
Bright before us
Like a flame.

Yesterday
A night-gone thing,
A sun-down name.

And dawn-today
Broad arch above the road we came.

Epilogue

I, too, sing America.

I am the darker brother.
They send me to eat in the kitchen
When company comes,
But I laugh,
And eat well,
And grow strong.

Tomorrow,
I'll sit at the table
When company comes.
Nobody'll dare
Say to me,
"Eat in the kitchen,"
Then.

Besides,
They'll see how beautiful I am
And be ashamed,—

I, too, am America.

Fine Clothes to the Jew

(1927)

To Carl Van Vechten

Poetry, Vanity Fair, Opportunity, The New Republic, The Measure, The Crisis, The New Masses, The Buccaneer, The Messenger, Books of the New *York Herald Tribune, Fire!!, The Lincoln News, Palms,* and *The Modern Quarterly* have first published some of these poems. The author thanks them for permission to reprint.

Contents

A Note on Blues

The first eight and the last nine poems in this book are written after the manner of the Negro folk-songs known as *Blues*. The *Blues*, unlike the *Spirituals*, have a strict poetic pattern: one long line repeated and a third line to rhyme with the first two. Sometimes the second line in repetition is slightly changed and sometimes, but very seldom, it is omitted. The mood of the *Blues* is almost always despondency, but when they are sung people laugh.

Blues

Hey!

Sun's a settin',
This is what I'm gonna sing.
Sun's a settin',
This is what I'm gonna sing:
I feels de blues a comin',
Wonder what de blues'll bring?

Hard Luck

When hard luck overtakes you
Nothin' for you to do.
When hard luck overtakes you
Nothin' for you to do.
Gather up yo' fine clothes
An' sell 'em to de Jew.

Jew takes yo' fine clothes,
Gives you a dollar an' a half.
Jew takes yo' fine clothes,
Gives you a dollar an' a half.
Go to de bootleg's,
Git some gin to make you laugh.

If I was a mule I'd
Git me a waggon to haul.
If I was a mule I'd
Git a waggon to haul.
I'm so low-down I
Ain't even got a stall.

Misery

Play de blues for me.
Play de blues for me.
No other music
'Ll ease ma misery.

Sing a soothin' song.
Said a soothin' song,
Cause de man I love's done
Done me wrong.

Can't you understand,
O, understand
A good woman's cryin'
For a no-good man?

Black gal like me,
Black gal like me
'S got to hear a blues
For her misery.

Suicide

Ma sweet good man has
Packed his trunk and left.
Ma sweet good man has
Packed his trunk and left.
Nobody to love me:
I'm gonna kill ma self.

I'm gonna buy me a knife with
A blade ten inches long.
Gonna buy a knife with
A blade ten inches long.

Shall I carve ma self or
That man that done me wrong?

'Lieve I'll jump in de river
Eighty-nine feet deep.
'Lieve I'll jump in de river
Eighty-nine feet deep.
Cause de river's quiet
An' a po', po' gal can sleep.

Bad Man

I'm a bad, bad man
Cause everbody tells me so.
I'm a bad, bad man.
Everbody tells me so.
I takes ma meanness and ma licker
Everwhere I go.

I beats ma wife an'
I beats ma side gal too.
Beats ma wife an'
Beats ma side gal too.
Don't know why I do it but
It keeps me from feelin' blue.

I'm so bad I
Don't even want to be good.
So bad, bad, bad I
Don't even want to be good.
I'm goin' to de devil an'
I wouldn't go to heaben if I could.

Gypsy Man

Ma man's a gypsy
Cause he never does come home.
Ma man's a gypsy,—
He never does come home.
I'm gonna be a gypsy woman
Fer I can't stay here alone.

Once I was in Memphis,
I mean Tennessee.
Once I was in Memphis,
Said Tennessee.
But I had to leave cause
Nobody there was good to me.

I met a yellow papa,
He took ma last thin dime.
Met a yellow papa,
He took ma last thin dime.
I give it to him cause I loved him
But I'll have mo' sense next time.

Love, Oh, love is
Such a strange disease.
Love, Oh, love is
Such a strange disease.
When it hurts yo' heart you
Sho can't find no ease.

Po' Boy Blues

When I was home de
Sunshine seemed like gold.
When I was home de

Sunshine seemed like gold.
Since I come up North de
Whole damn world's turned cold.

I was a good boy,
Never done no wrong.
Yes, I was a good boy,
Never done no wrong,
But this world is weary
An' de road is hard an' long.

I fell in love with
A gal I thought was kind.
Fell in love with
A gal I thought was kind.
She made me lose ma money
An' almost lose ma mind.

Weary, weary,
Weary early in de morn.
Weary, weary,
Early, early in de morn.
I's so weary
I wish I'd never been born.

Homesick Blues

De railroad bridge's
A sad song in de air.
De railroad bridge's
A sad song in de air.
Ever time de trains pass
I wants to go somewhere.

I went down to de station.
Ma heart was in ma mouth.
Went down to de station.
Heart was in ma mouth.
Lookin' for a box car
To roll me to de South.

Homesick blues, Lawd,
'S a terrible thing to have.
Homesick blues is
A terrible thing to have.
To keep from cryin'
I opens ma mouth an' laughs.

Railroad Avenue

Railroad Avenue

Dusk dark
On Railroad Avenue.
Lights in the fish joints,
Lights in the pool rooms.
A box-car some train
Has forgotten
In the middle of the
Block.
A player piano,
A victrola.
   942
   Was the number.
A boy
Lounging on a corner.
A passing girl
With purple powdered skin.
   Laughter
   Suddenly
   Like a taut drum.
   Laughter
   Suddenly
   Neither truth nor lie.
   Laughter
Hardening the dusk dark evening.
   Laughter
Shaking the lights in the fish joints,
Rolling white balls in the pool rooms,
And leaving untouched the box-car
Some train has forgotten.

Brass Spittoons

Clean the spitoons, boy.
   Detroit,
   Chicago,
   Atlantic City,
   Palm Beach.
Clean the spitoons.
The steam in hotel kitchens,
And the smoke in hotel lobbies,
And the slime in hotel spitoons:
Part of my life.
   Hey, boy!
   A nickel,
   A dime,
   A dollar,
Two dollars a day.
   Hey, boy!
   A nickel,
   A dime,
   A dollar,
   Two dollars
Buys shoes for the baby.
House rent to pay.
Gin on Saturday,
Church on Sunday.
   My God!
Babies and gin and church
and women and Sunday
all mixed up with dimes and
dollars and clean spitoons
and house rent to pay
   Hey, boy!
A bright bowl of brass is beautiful to the Lord.
Bright polished brass like the cymbals

Of King David's dancers,
Like the wine cups of Solomon.
   Hey, boy!
A clean spitoon on the altar of the Lord.
A clean bright spitoon all newly polished,—
At least I can offer that.
   Com' mere, boy!

Ruby Brown

She was young and beautiful
And golden like the sunshine
That warmed her body.
And because she was colored
Mayville had no place to offer her,
Nor fuel for the clean flame of joy
That tried to burn within her soul.

One day,
Sitting on old Mrs. Latham's back porch
Polishing the silver,
She asked herself two questions
And they ran something like this:
What can a colored girl do
On the money from a white woman's kitchen?
And ain't there any joy in this town?

Now the streets down by the river
Know more about this pretty Ruby Brown,
And the sinister shuttered houses of the bottoms
Hold a yellow girl
Seeking an answer to her questions.
The good church folk do not mention
Her name any more.

But the white men,
Habitués of the high shuttered houses,
Pay more money to her now
Than they ever did before,
When she worked in their kitchens.

The New Cabaret Girl

That little yaller gal
Wid blue-green eyes:
If her daddy ain't white
Would be a surprise.

She don't drink gin
An' she don't like corn.
I asked her one night
Where she was born.

An' she say, Honey,
I don't know
Where I come from
Or where I go.

That crazy little yaller gal
Wid blue-green eyes:
If her daddy ain't 'fay
Would be a surprise.

An' there she sets a cryin'
In de cabaret
A lookin' all sad
When she ought to play.

My God, I says,
You can't live that way!

Babe, you can't
Live that way!

Closing Time

Starter!

> Her face is pale
> In the doorway light.
> Her lips blood red
> And her skin blue white.

Taxi!

> I'm tired.

Deep . . . River. . . .

> O, God, please!

The river and the moon hold memories.

> Comets play.
> Dancers whirl.
> Death, be kind.

What was the cover charge, kid?

> To a little drowned girl.

Prize Fighter

Only dumb guys fight.
> If I wasn't dumb
> I wouldn't be fightin'.
> I could make six dollars a day

On the docks
   And I'd save more than I do now.
Only dumb guys fight.

Crap Game

Lemme roll 'em, boy.
I got ma tail curled!
If a seven don't come
'Leven ain't far away.
An' if I craps,
Dark baby,
Trouble
Don't last all de time.
Hit 'em, bones!

Ballad of Gin Mary

Carried me to de court,
Judge was settin' there.
Looked all around me,
Didn't have a friend nowhere.

Judge Pierce he says, Mary.
Old Judge says, Mary Jane,
Ever time I mounts this bench
I sees yo' face again.

O, Lawd! O, Lawd!
O, Lawd . . . Lawdee!
Seems like bad licker,
Judge, won't let me be.

Old Judge says you's a drunkard.
Fact is you worries me.
Gwine give you eighteen months
So licker'll let you be.

Eighteen months in jail!
O, eighteen months locked in!
Won't be so bad in jail
But I'll miss ma gin.

O, please sir, Judge, have mercy!
Have mercy, please, on me!
Old hard-faced Judge says eighteen months
Till licker'll let you be.

Death of Do Dirty: A Rounder's Song

O, you can't find a buddy
Any old time
'Ll help you out
When you ain't got a dime.

He was a friend o' mine.

They called him Do Dirty
Cause he was black
An' had cut his gal
An' shot a man in de back.

Ma friend o' mine.

But when I was hungry,
Had nothin' to eat,
He bought me corn bread
An' a stew o' meat.

Good friend o' mine.

An' when de cops got me
An' put me in jail
If Dirty had de money
He'd go ma bail.

O, friend o' mine.

That night he got kilt
I was standin' in de street.
Somebody comes by
An' says yo' boy is gettin' beat.

Ma friend o' mine.

But when I got there
An' seen de ambulance
A guy was sayin'
He ain't got a chance.

Best friend o' mine.

An' de ones that kilt him,—
Damn their souls,—
I'm gonna fill 'em up full o'
Bullet holes.

Ma friend o' mine.

Elevator Boy

I got a job now
Runnin' an elevator
In the Dennison Hotel in Jersey.

Job ain't no good though.
No money around.
    Jobs are just chances
    Like everthing else.
    Maybe a little luck now,
    Maybe not.
    Maybe a good job sometimes:
    Step out o' the barrel, boy.
Two new suits an'
A woman to sleep with.
    Maybe no luck for a long time.
    Only the elevators
    Goin' up an' down,
    Up an' down,
    Or somebody else's shoes
    To shine,
    Or greasy pots in a dirty kitchen.
I been runnin' this
Elevator too long.
Guess I'll quit now.

Porter

I must say
Yes, sir,
To you all the time.
Yes, sir!
Yes, sir!
All my days
Climbing up a great big mountain
Of yes, sirs!

Rich old white man
Owns the world.
Gimme yo' shoes
To shine.

Yes, sir!

Sport

Life
For him
Must be
The shivering of
A great drum
Beaten with swift sticks
Then at the closing hour
The lights go out
And there is no music at all
And death becomes
An empty cabaret
And eternity an unblown saxophone
And yesterday
A glass of gin
Drunk long
Ago.

Saturday Night

Play it once.
O, play some more.
Charlie is a gambler
An' Sadie is a whore.
    A glass o' whiskey

An' a glass o' gin:
Strut, Mr. Charlie,
Till de dawn comes in.
Pawn yo' gold watch
An' diamond ring.
Git a quart o' licker,
Let's shake dat thing!
Skee-de-dad! De-dad!
Doo-doo-doo!
Won't be nothin' left
When de worms git through
An' you's a long time
Dead
When you is
Dead, too.
So beat dat drum, boy!
Shout dat song:
Shake 'em up an' shake 'em up
All night long.
Hey! Hey!
Ho . . . Hum!
Do, it, Mr. Charlie,
Till de red dawn come.

Glory! Halleluiah!

Judgment Day

They put ma body in de ground,
Ma soul went flyin' o' de town.

Lord Jesus!

Went flyin' to de stars an' moon
A shoutin' God, I's comin' soon.

O Jesus!

Lord in heaben,
Crown on His head,
Says don't be 'fraid
Cause you ain't dead.

Kind Jesus!

An' now I'm settin' clean an' bright
In de sweet o' ma Lord's sight,—
   Clean an' bright,
     Clean an' bright.

Prayer Meeting

Glory! Halleluiah!
De dawn's a-comin'!
Glory! Halleluiah!
De dawn's a-comin'!
A black old woman croons
In the amen-corner of the

Ebecanezer Baptist Church.
A black old woman croons,—
De dawn's a-comin'!

Feet o' Jesus

At de feet o' Jesus,
Sorrow like a sea.
Lordy, let yo' mercy
Come driftin' down on me.

At de feet o' Jesus,
At yo' feet I stand.
O, ma little Jesus,
Please reach out yo' hand.

Prayer

I ask you this:
Which way to go?
I ask you this:
Which sin to bear?
Which crown to put
Upon my hair?
I do not know,
Lord God,
I do not know.

Shout

Listen to yo' prophets,
  Little Jesus!
Listen to yo' saints!

Fire

Fire,
Fire, Lord!
Fire gonna burn ma soul!

I ain't been good,
I ain't been clean,—
I been stinkin', low-down, mean.

Fire,
Fire, Lord!
Fire gonna burn ma soul!

Tell me, brother,
Do you believe
If you wanta go to heaben
Got to moan an' grieve?

Fire,
Fire, Lord!
Fire gonna burn ma soul!

I been stealin',
Been tellin' lies,
Had more women
Than Pharaoh had wives.

Fire,
Fire, Lord!

Fire gonna burn ma soul!
I means Fire, Lord!
Fire gonna burn ma soul!

Moan

I'm deep in trouble,
Nobody to understand,
   Lord, Lord!

Deep in trouble,
Nobody to understand,
   O, Lord!

Gonna pray to ma Jesus,
Ask him to gimme His hand.
   Ma Lord!

I'm moanin', moanin',
Nobody cares just why.
   No, Lord!

Moanin', moanin',
Feels like I could die.
   O, Lord!

Sho, there must be peace,
   Ma Jesus,
Somewhere in yo' sky.
   Yes, Lord!

Angels Wings

De angels wings is white as snow,
  O, white as snow,
      White
           as
              snow.
De angels wings is white as snow,
  But I drug ma wings
  In de dirty mire.
  O, I drug ma wings
  All through de fire.
But de angels wings is white as snow,
      White
           as
              snow.

Sinner

Have mercy, Lord!

Po' an' black
An' humble an' lonesome
An' a sinner in yo' sight.

Have mercy, Lord!

Beale Street Love

Beale Street Love

Love
Is a brown man's fist
With hard knuckles
Crushing the lips,
Blackening the eyes,—
Hit me again,
Says Clorinda.

Cora

I broke ma heart this mornin'.
Ain't got no heart no mo'.
Next time a man comes near me
Gonna shut an' lock ma door
Cause they treats me mean,—
The ones I loves.
They always treats me mean.

Workin' Man

I works all day
Wid a pick an' a shovel.
Comes home at night,—
It ain't nothin' but a hovel.

I calls for ma woman
When I opens de door.

She's out in de street,—
Ain't nothin' but a 'hore.

I does her good
An' I treats her fine,
But she don't gimme lovin'
Cause she ain't de right kind.

I'm a hard workin' man
An' I sho pays double
Cause I tries to be good
An' gits nothin' but trouble.

Bad Luck Card

Cause you don't love me
Is awful, awful hard.
Gypsy done showed me
Ma bad luck card.

There ain't no good left
In this world for me.
Gypsy done tole me,—
Unlucky as can be.

I don't know what
Po' weary me can do.
Gypsy says I'd kill ma self
If I was you.

Baby

Albert!
Hey, Albert!

Don't you play in dat road.
   You see dem trucks
   A goin' by.
   One run ovah you
   An' you die.
Albert, don't you play in dat road.

Evil Woman

I ain't gonna mistreat ma
Good gal any more.
I'm just gonna kill her
Next time she makes me sore.

I treats her kind but
She don't do me right.
She fights an' quarrels most
Ever night.

I can't have no woman's
Got such low-down ways,
Cause a blue-gummed woman
Ain't de style now days.

I brought her from de South
An' she's goin' on back
Else I'll use her head
For a carpet tack.

A Ruined Gal

Standin' by de lonesome riverside
After de boat's done gone,
   Po' weary me

Won't be nobody's bride
Cause I is long gone wrong.

Standin' by de weary riverside
When de boat comes in,
   Po' lonesome me
   Won't meet nobody
   Cause I ain't got no friend.

By de edge o' de weary riverside
Night-time's comin' down.
   Ain't nothin' for a ruined gal
   But jump overboard an' drown.

O, de lonesome riverside,
O, de wicked water.
   Damn ma black old mammy's soul
   For ever havin' a daughter.

Minnie Sings Her Blues

Cabaret, cabaret!
That's where ma man an' me go.
Cabaret, cabaret!
That's where we go,—
Leaves de snow outside
An' our troubles at de door.

Jazz band, jazz band!
Ma man an' me dance.
When I cuddles up to him
No other gal's got a chance.

Baby, O, Baby,
I'm midnight mad.

If ma daddy didn't love me
It sho would be sad.
If he didn't love me
I'd go away
An' dig me a grave this very day.

Blues . . . blues!
Blue, blue, blues!
I'd sho have them blues.

Dressed Up

I had ma clothes cleaned
Just like new.
I put 'em on but
I still feels blue.

I bought a new hat,
Sho is fine,
But I wish I had back that
Old gal o' mine.

I got new shoes,—
They don't hurt ma feet,
But I ain't got nobody
For to call me sweet.

Black Gal

I's always been a workin' girl.
I treated Albert fine.
Ain't cut him wid no razor,
Ain't never been unkind.

Yet it seems like always
Men takes all they can from me
Then they goes an' finds a yaller gal
An' lets me be.

I dressed up Albert Johnson.
I bought him suits o' clothes,
An' soon as he got out de barrel
Then out ma door he goes.

Yet I ain't never been no bad one.
Can't help it cause I'm black.
I hates them rinney yaller gals
An' I wants ma Albert back.
Ma little, short, sweet, brownskin boy,—
Oh, God, I wants him back!

From the Georgia Roads

Sun Song

Sun and softness,
Sun and the beaten hardness of the earth,
Sun and the song of all the sun-stars
Gathered together,—
Dark ones of Africa,
I bring you my songs
To sing on the Georgia roads.

Magnolia Flowers

The quiet fading out of life
In a corner full of ugliness.

I went lookin' for magnolia flowers
But I didn't find 'em.
I went lookin' for magnolia flowers in the dusk
And there was only this corner
Full of ugliness.

   'Scuse me,
   I didn't mean to stump ma toe on you, lady.

There ought to be magnolias
Somewhere in this dusk.

   'Scuse me,
   I didn't mean to stump ma toe on you.

Mulatto

    I am your son, white man!

Georgia dusk
And the turpentine woods.
One of the pillars of the temple fell.

    You are my son!
    Like hell!

The moon over the turpentine woods.
The Southern night
Full of stars,
Great big yellow stars.
      Juicy bodies
      Of nigger wenches
      Blue black
      Against black fences.
      O, you little bastard boy,
      What's a body but a toy?
The scent of pine wood stings the soft night air.
    What's the body of your mother?
Silver moonlight everywhere.
    What's the body of your mother?
Sharp pine scent in the evening air.
      A nigger night,
      A nigger joy,
      A little yellow
      Bastard boy.

    Naw, you ain't my brother.
    Niggers ain't my brother.
    Not ever.
    Niggers ain't my brother.

The Southern night is full of stars,
Great big yellow stars.
 O, sweet as earth,
 Dusk dark bodies
 Give sweet birth
To little yellow bastard boys.

 Git on back there in the night,
 You ain't white.

The bright stars scatter everywhere.
Pine wood scent in the evening air.
 A nigger night,
 A nigger joy.

 I am your son, white man!

 A little yellow
 Bastard boy.

Red Silk Stockings

Put on yo' red silk stockings,
Black gal.
Go out an' let de white boys
Look at yo' legs.

Ain't nothin' to do for you, nohow,
Round this town,—
You's too pretty.
Put on yo' red silk stockings, gal,
An' tomorrow's chile'll
Be a high yaller.

Go out an' let de white boys
Look at yo' legs.

Jazz Band in a Parisian Cabaret

Play that thing,
Jazz band!
Play it for the lords and ladies,
For the dukes and counts,
For the whores and gigolos,
For the American millionaires,
And the school teachers
Out for a spree.
Play it,
Jazz band!
You know that tune
That laughs and cries at the same time.
You know it.
   May I?
   Mais oui.
   Mien Gott!
   Parece una rumba.
Play it, jazz band!
You've got seven languages to speak in
And then some,
Even if you do come from Georgia.
   Can I go home wid yuh, sweetie?
   Sure.

Song for a Dark Girl

Way Down South in Dixie
  (Break the heart of me)
They hung my black young lover
  To a cross roads tree.

Way Down South in Dixie
   (Bruised body high in air)
I asked the white Lord Jesus
   What was the use of prayer.

Way Down South in Dixie
   (Break the heart of me)
Love is a naked shadow
   On a gnarled and naked tree.

Mammy

I'm waiting for ma mammy,—
   She is Death.

Say it very softly.
Say it very slowly if you choose.

I'm waiting for ma mammy,—
   Death.

Laughers

Dream singers,
Story tellers,
Dancers,
Loud laughers in the hands of Fate—
   My people.
Dish-washers,
Elevator-boys,
Ladies' maids,
Crap-shooters,
Cooks,
Waiters,

Jazzers,
Nurses of babies,
Loaders of ships,
Rounders,
Number writers,
Comedians in vaudeville
And band-men in circuses—
Dream-singers all,—
    My people.
Story-tellers all,—
    My people.
    Dancers—
God! What dancers!
    Singers—
God! What singers!
Singers and dancers.
Dancers and laughers.
    Laughers?
Yes, laughers . . . laughers . . . laughers—
Loud-mouthed laughers in the hands
    Of Fate.

And Blues

Lament over Love

I hope ma chile'll
Never love a man.
I say I hope ma chile'll
Never love a man.
Cause love can hurt you
Mo'n anything else can.

I'm goin' down to de river
An' I ain't goin' there to swim.
Goin' down to de river,
Ain't goin' there to swim.
Ma true love's left me, an'
I'm goin' there to think about him.

Love is like whiskey,
Love is like red, red wine.
Love is like whiskey,
O, like sweet red wine.
If you wants to be happy
You got to love all de time.

I'm goin' up in a tower
Tall as a tree is tall.
Say up in a tower
Tall as a tree is tall.
Gonna think about ma man an'
Let ma fool-self fall.

Gal's Cry for a Dying Lover

Heard de owl a hootin',
Knowed somebody's 'bout to die.
Heard de owl a hootin',
Knowed somebody's 'bout to die.
Put ma head un'neath de kiver,
Started in to moan an' cry.

Hound dawg's barkin'
Means he's gonna leave this world.
Hound dawg's barkin'
Means he's gonna leave this world.
O, Lawd have mercy
On a po' black girl.

Black an' ugly
But he sho do treat me kind.
I'm black an' ugly
But he sho do treat me kind.
High-in-heaben Jesus,
Please don't take this man o' mine.

Young Gal's Blues

I'm gonna walk to de graveyard
'Hind ma friend Miss Cora Lee.
Gonna walk to de graveyard
'Hind ma dear friend Cora Lee
Cause when I'm dead some
Body'll have to walk behind me.

I'm goin' to de po' house
To see ma old Aunt Clew.
Goin' to de po' house

To see ma old Aunt Clew.
When I'm old an' ugly
I'll want to see somebody, too.

De po' house is lonely
An' de grave is cold.
O, de po' house is lonely,
De graveyard grave is cold.
But I'd rather be dead than
To be ugly an' old.

When love is gone what
Can a young gal do?
When love is gone, O,
What can a young gal do?
Keep on a-lovin' me, daddy,
Cause I don't want to be blue.

Midwinter Blues

In de middle of de winter,
Snow all over de ground.
In de middle of de winter,
Snow all over de ground,—
'Twas de night befo' Christmas
Ma good man turned me down.

Don' know's I'd mind his goin'
But he left me when de coal was low.
Don' know's I'd mind his goin'
But he left when de coal was low.
Now, if a man loves a woman
That ain't no time to go.

He told me that he loved me
But he must a been tellin' a lie.
He told me that he loved me.
He must a been tellin' a lie.
But he's the only man I'll
Love till de day I die.

I'm gonna buy me a rose bud
An' plant it at ma back door.
Gonna buy me a rose bud
And plant it at ma back door,
So when I'm dead they
Won't need no flowers from de store.

Listen Here Blues

Sweet girls, sweet girls,
Listen here to me.
All you sweet girls,
Listen here to me:
Gin an' whiskey
Kin make you lose yo' 'ginity.

I used to be a good chile,
Lawd, in Sunday School.
Used to be a good chile,—
Always in Sunday School,
Till these licker-headed rounders
Made me everbody's fool.

Good girls, good girls,
Listen here to me.
Oh, you good girls,
Better listen to me:

Don't you fool wid no men cause
They'll bring you misery.

Hard Daddy

I went to ma daddy,
Says Daddy I have got de blues.
Went to ma daddy,
Says Daddy I have got de blues.
Ma daddy says Honey
Can't you bring no better news?

I cried on his shoulder but
He turned his back on me.
Cried on his shoulder but
He turned his back on me.
He said a woman's cryin's
Never gonna bother me.

I wish I had wings to
Fly like de eagle flies.
Wish I had wings to
Fly like de eagle flies.
I'd fly on ma man an'
I'd scratch out both his eyes.

Bound No'th Blues

Goin' down de road, Lawd,
Goin' down de road.
Down de road, Lawd,
Way, way down de road.

Got to find somebody
To help me carry dis load.

Road's in front o' me,
Nothin' to do but walk.
Road's in front o' me,
Walk . . . and walk . . . and walk.
I'd like to meet a good friend
To come along an' talk.

Hates to be lonely,
Lawd, I hates to be sad.
Says I hates to be lonely,
Hates to be lonely an' sad,
But ever friend you finds seems
Like they try to do you bad.

Road, road, road, O!
Road, road . . . road . . . road, road!
Road, road, road, O!
On de No'thern road.
These Mississippi towns ain't
Fit fer a hoppin' toad.

Ma Man

When ma man looks at me
He knocks me off ma feet.
When ma man looks at me
He knocks me off ma feet.
He's got those 'lectric-shockin' eyes an'
De way he shocks me sho is sweet.

He kin play a banjo.
Lordy, he kin plunk, plunk, plunk.

He kin play a banjo.
I mean plunk, plunk . . . plunk, plunk.
He plays good when he's sober
An' better, better, better when he's drunk.

Eagle-rockin',
Daddy, eagle-rock with me.
Eagle rockin',
Come an' eagle-rock with me.
Honey baby,
Eagle-rockish as I kin be!

Hey! Hey!

Sun's a risin',
This is gonna be ma song.
Sun's a risin',
This is gonna be ma song.
I could be blue but
I been blue all night long.

Dear Lovely Death

(1931)

Contents

Drum

Bear in mind
That death is a drum
Beating for ever
Till the last worms come
To answer its call,
Till the last stars fall,
Until the last atom
Is no atom at all,
Until time is lost
And there is no air
And space itself
Is nothing nowhere.
Death is a drum,
A signal drum,
Calling all life
To Come! Come!
Come!

The Consumptive

All day in the sun
That he loved so
He sat,
Feeling life go.

All night in bed
Waiting for sleep
He lay,
Feeling death creep—
Creeping like fire

Creeping like fire from a slow spark
Choking his breath
And burning the dark.

Dear Lovely Death

Dear lovely Death
That taketh all things under wing—
Never to kill—
Only to change
Into some other thing
This suffering flesh,
To make it either more or less,
But not again the same—
Dear lovely Death,
Change is thy other name.

Tower

Death is a tower
To which the soul ascends
To spend a meditative hour—
That never ends.

Two Things

Two things possess the power,
Two things deserve the name,
Two things can reawaken
Perpetually the flame.
Two things are full of wonder,
Two things cast off all shame.

One is known by the name of Death.
And the other has no name
Except the name each gives it—
In no single mouth the same.

Flight

Plant your toes in the cool swamp mud.
Step and leave no track.
Hurry, sweating runner!
The hounds are at your back.

"No I didn't touch her
White flesh ain't for me".

Hurry! Black boy, hurry!
They'll swing you to a tree.

Afro-American Fragment

So long,
So far away,
Is Africa.
Not even memories alive
Save those that history books create,
Save those that songs beat back into the blood—
Beat out of blood with words sad sung
In strange un-Negro tongue—
So long,
So far away
Is Africa.

Subdued and time lost are the drums—
And yet, through some vast mist of race

There comes this song
I do not understand,
This song of atavistic land,
Of bitter yearnings lost, without a place—
So long,
So far away
Is Africa's
Dark face.

Demand

Listen!
Dear dream of utter aliveness—
Touching my body of utter death—
Tell me, o quickly! dream of aliveness,
The flaming source of your bright breath.
Tell me, O dream of utter aliveness—
Knowing so well the wind and the sun
    Where is this light
    Your eyes see forever?
    And what is this wind
    You touch when you run?

Sailor

He sat upon the rolling deck
Half a world away from home,
And smoked a Capstan cigarette
And watched the blue waves tipped
   with foam.

He had a mermaid on his arm,
An anchor on his breast,

And tattooed on his back he had
A blue bird in a nest.

Florida Road Workers

I'm makin' a road
For the cars
To fly by on.
Makin' a road
Through the palmetto thicket
For light and civilization
To travel on.

Makin' a road
For the rich old white men
To sweep over in their big cars
And leave me standin' here.

Sure,
A road helps all of us!
White folks ride—
And I get to see 'em ride.
I ain't never seen nobody
Ride so fine before.
Hey buddy!
Look at me!
I'm making a road!

Poem

Strange,
Distorted blades of grass,
Strange,

Distorted trees,
Strange,
Distorted tulips on their knees.

Aesthete in Harlem

Strange,
That in this nigger place,
I should meet Life face to face
When for years, I had been seeking
Life in places gentler speaking
Until I came to this near street
And found Life—stepping on my feet!

A New Song

(1938)

Contents

Let America Be America Again

Let America be America again.
Let it be the dream it used to be.
Let it be the pioneer on the plain
Seeking a home where he himself is free.

(America never was America to me.)

Let America be the dream the dreamers dreamed—
Let it be that great strong land of love
Where never kings connive nor tyrants scheme
That any man be crushed by one above.

(It never was America to me.)

O, let my land be a land where Liberty
Is crowned with no false patriotic wreath,
But opportunity is real, and life is free,
Equality is in the air we breathe.

(There's never been equality for me,
Nor freedom in this "homeland of the free.")

Say who are you that mumbles in the dark?
And who are you that draws your veil across the stars?

I am the poor white, fooled and pushed apart,
I am the Negro bearing slavery's scars.
I am the red man driven from the land,
I am the immigrant clutching the hope I seek—
And finding only the same old stupid plan.
Of dog eat dog, of mighty crush the weak.

I am the young man, full of strength and hope,
Tangled in that ancient endless chain
Of profit, power, gain, of grab the land!

Of grab the gold! Of grab the ways of satisfying need!
Of work the men! Of take the pay!
Of owning everything for one's own greed!

I am the farmer, bondsman to the soil.
I am the worker sold to the machine.
I am the Negro, servant to you all.
I am the people, humble, hungry, mean—
I am the man who never got ahead,
The poorest worker bartered through the years.

Yet I'm the one who dreamt our basic dream
In that Old World while still a serf of kings,
Who dreamt a dream so strong, so brave, so true,
That even yet its mighty daring sings
In every brick and stone, in every furrow turned
That's made America the land it has become.
O, I'm the man who sailed those early seas
In search of what I meant to be my home—
For I'm the one who left dark Ireland's shore,
And Poland's plain, and England's grassy lea,
And torn from Black Africa's strand I came
To build a "homeland of the free."

The free?

Who said the free? Not me?
Surely not me? The millions on relief today?
The millions shot down when we strike?
The millions who have nothing for our pay?
For all the dreams we've dreamed
And all the songs we've sung
And all the hopes we've held
And all the flags we've hung,
The millions who have nothing for our pay—
Except the dream that's almost dead today.

O, let America be America again—
The land that never has been yet—
And yet must be—the land where *every* man is free.
The land that's mine—the poor man's, Indian's, Negro's, ME—
Who made America,
Whose sweat and blood, whose faith and pain,
Whose hand at the foundry, whose plow in the rain,
Must bring back our mighty dream again.

Sure, call me any ugly name you choose—
From those who live like leeches on the people's lives,
We must take back our land again,
America!

O, yes,
I say it plain,
America never was America to me,
And yet I swear this oath—
America will be!

Out of the rack and ruin of our gangster death,
The rape and rot of graft, and stealth, and lies,
We, the people, must redeem
The land, the mines, the plants, the rivers,
The mountains and the endless plain—
All, all the stretch of these great green states—
And make America again!

Justice

That Justice is a blind goddess
Is a thing to which we poor are wise:
Her bandage hides two festering sores
That once perhaps were eyes.

Park Bench

I live on a park bench.
You, Park Avenue.
Hell of a distance
Between us two.

I beg a dime for dinner—
You got a butler and maid.
But I'm wakin' up!
Say, ain't you afraid

That I might, just maybe,
In a year or two,
Move on over
To Park Avenue?

Chant for Tom Mooney

Tom Mooney!
Tom Mooney!
Tom Mooney!
A man with the title of governor has spoken:
And you do not go free.
A man with the title of governor has spoken:
And the steel bars surround you,
And the prison walls wrap you about,
And you do not go free.
But the man with the title of governor
Does not know
That all over the earth today
The workers speak the name:
Tom Mooney!
Tom Mooney!
Tom Mooney!

And the sound vibrates in waves
    From Africa to China,
    India to Germany,
    Russia to the Argentine,
    Shaking the bars,
    Shaking the walls,
    Shaking the earth
Until the whole world falls into the hands of
    The workers.
Of course, the man with the title of governor
Will be forgotten then
On the scrap heap of time—
He won't matter at all.
But remembered forever will be the name:
    TOM MOONEY.
    Schools will be named:
    TOM MOONEY.
    Farms will be named:
    TOM MOONEY.
    Dams will be named:
    TOM MOONEY.
    Ships will be named:
    TOM MOONEY.
    Factories will be named:
    TOM MOONEY.
    And all over the world—
Banner of force and labor, strength and union,
Life forever through the workers' power—
    Will be the name:
    TOM MOONEY.

Chant for May Day

To be read by a Workman with, for background, the rhythmic waves of
rising and re-rising Mass Voices, multiplying like the roar of the sea.

WORKER:	The first of May:
	When the flowers break through the earth,
	When the sap rises in the trees,
	When the birds come back from the South.
	Workers:
	Be like the flowers,
10 VOICES:	Bloom in the strength of your unknown power,
20 VOICES:	Grow out of the passive earth,
40 VOICES:	Grow strong with Union,
	All hands together—
	To beautify this hour, this spring,
	And all the springs to come
50 VOICES:	Forever for the workers!
WORKER:	Workers:
10 VOICES:	Be like the sap rising in the trees,
20 VOICES:	Strengthening each branch,
40 VOICES:	No part neglected—
50 VOICES:	Reaching all the world.
WORKER:	All workers:
10 VOICES:	White workers,
10 OTHERS:	Black workers,
10 OTHERS:	Yellow workers,
10 OTHERS:	Workers in the islands of the sea—
50 VOICES:	Life is everywhere for you,
WORKER:	When the sap of your own strength rises
50 VOICES:	Life is everywhere.
10 VOICES:	May Day!
20 VOICES:	May Day!
40 VOICES:	May Day!
50 VOICES:	When the earth is new,
WORKER:	Proletarians of all the world:
20 VOICES:	Arise,
40 VOICES:	Grow strong,
60 VOICES:	Take Power,
80 VOICES:	Till the forces of the earth are yours
100 VOICES:	From this hour.

Pride

Let all who will
Eat quietly the bread of shame.
I cannot,
Without complaining loud and long,
Tasting its bitterness in my throat,
And feeling to my very soul
It's wrong.
For honest work
You proffer me poor pay,
For honest dreams
Your spit is in my face,
And so my fist is clenched—
Today—
To strike your face.

Ballad of Ozie Powell

Red is the Alabama road,
    Ozie, Ozie Powell,
Redder now where your blood has flowed,
    Ozie, Ozie Powell.

Strong are the bars and steel the gate,
    Ozie, Ozie Powell,
The High Sheriff's eyes are filled with hate,
    Ozie, Ozie Powell.

The High Sheriff shoots and he shoots to kill
    Black young Ozie Powell.
The Law's a Klansman with an evil will,
    Ozie, Ozie Powell.

Nine old men in Washington,
    Ozie, Ozie Powell,
Never saw the High Sheriff's gun
    Aimed at Ozie Powell.

Nine old men so rich and wise,
    Ozie, Ozie Powell,
They never saw the High Sheriff's eyes
    Stare at Ozie Powell.

But nine black boys know full well,
    Don't they, Ozie Powell?
What it is to live in hell,
    Ozie, Ozie Powell.

The devil's a Kleagle with an evil will,
    Ozie, Ozie Powell,
A white High Sheriff who shoots to kill
    Black young Ozie Powell.

And red is that Alabama road,
    Ozie, Ozie Powell,
But redder now where your life's blood flowed,
    Ozie! Ozie Powell!

Kids Who Die

This is for the kids who die,
Black and white,
For kids will die certainly.
The old and rich will live on awhile,
As always,
Eating blood and gold,
Letting kids die.

Kids will die in the swamps of Mississippi
Organizing sharecroppers.
Kids will die in the streets of Chicago
Organizing workers.
Kids will die in the orange groves of California
Telling others to get together.
Whites and Filipinos,
Negroes and Mexicans,
All kinds of kids will die
Who don't believe in lies, and bribes, and contentment,
And a lousy peace.

Of course, the wise and the learned
Who pen editorials in the papers,
And the gentlemen with Dr. in front of their names,
White and black,
Who make surveys and write books,
Will live on weaving words to smother the kids who die,
And the sleazy courts,
And the bribe-reaching police,
And the blood-loving generals,
And the money-loving preachers
Will all raise their hands against the kids who die,
Beating them with laws and clubs and bayonets and bullets
To frighten the people—
For the kids who die are like iron in the blood of the people—
And the old and rich don't want the people
To taste the iron of the kids who die,
Don't want the people to get wise to their own power,
To believe an Angelo Herndon, or ever get together.

Listen, kids who die—
Maybe, now, there will be no monument for you
Except in our hearts.
Maybe your bodies'll be lost in a swamp,

Or a prison grave, or the potter's field,
Or the rivers where you're drowned like Liebknecht,
But the day will come—
You are sure yourselves that it is coming—
When the marching feet of the masses
Will raise for you a living monument of love,
And joy, and laughter,
And black bands and white hands clasped as one,
And a song that reaches the sky—
The song of the new life triumphant
Through the kids who die.

History

The past has been
A mint of blood and sorrow—
That must not be
True of tomorrow.

Ballads of Lenin

Comrade Lenin of Russia,
High in a marble tomb,
Move over, Comrade Lenin,
And give me room.

> I am Ivan, the peasant,
> Boots all muddy with soil.
> I fought with you, Comrade Lenin.
> Now I have finished my toil.

Comrade Lenin of Russia,
Alive in a marble tomb,

Move over, Comrade Lenin,
And make me room.

    I am Chico, the Negro,
    Cutting cane in the sun.
    I lived for you, Comrade Lenin.
    Now my work is done.

Comrade Lenin of Russia,
Honored in a marble tomb,
Move over, Comrade Lenin,
And leave me room.

    I am Chang from the foundries
    On strike in the streets of Shanghai.
    For the sake of the Revolution
    I fight, I starve, I die.

Comrade Lenin of Russia
Speaks from the marble:
On guard with the workers forever—
The world is our room!

Song of Spain

Come now, all you who are singers,
And sing me the song of Spain.
Sing it very simply that I might understand.

    What is the song of Spain?

Flamenco is the song of Spain:
Gypsies, guitars, dancing
Death and love and heartbreak
To a heel tap and a swirl of fingers

On three strings.
Flamenco is the song of Spain.

   I do not understand.

Toros are the song of Spain:
The bellowing bull, the red cape,
A sword thrust, a horn tip,
The torn suit of satin and gold,
Blood on the sand
Is the song of Spain.

   I do not understand.

Pintura is the song of Spain:
Goya, Velasquez, Murillo,
Splash of color on canvass,
Whirl of cherub-faces.
La Maja Desnuda's
The song of Spain.

   What's that?

Don Quixote! España!
Aquel rincon de la Mancha de
Cuyo nombre no quiero acordarme. . . .
That's the song of Spain.

   You wouldn't kid me, would you?
   A bombing plane's
   The song of Spain.
   Bullets like rain's
   The song of Spain.
   Poison gas is Spain.
   A knife in the back
   And its terror and pain is Spain.

Toros, flamenco, paintings, books—
    Not Spain.
The people are Spain:
The people beneath that bombing plane
With its wings of gold for which I pay—
I, a worker, letting my labor pile
Up millions for bombs to kill a child—
I bought those bombs for Spain!
Workers made those bombs for a Fascist Spain!
Will I make them again, and yet again?
    Storm clouds move fast.
    Our sky is gray.
    The white devils of the terror
    Await their day
When bombs'll fall not only on Spain—
    But on me and you!

Workers, make no bombs again!
Workers, mine no gold again!
Workers, lift no hand again
To build up profits for the rape of Spain!
Workers, see yourselves as Spain!
Workers, know that we too can cry,
Lift arms in vain, run, hide, die:
    Too late!
    The bombing plane!
Workers, make no bombs again
Except that they be made for us
    To hold and guard
Lest some Franco steal into our backyard
Under the guise of a patriot
Waving a flag and mouthing rot
And dropping bombs from a Christian steeple
    On the people.

I made those bombs for Spain.
I must not do it again.
I made those bombing planes.
I must not do it again.

I made rich the grandees and lords
Who hire Franco to lead his gang-hordes
Against Spain.

I must never do that again.

I must drive the bombers out of Spain!
I must drive the bombers out of the world!
I must take the world for my own again—

A workers' world
Is the song of Spain.

A New Song

I speak in the name of the black millions
Awakening to action.
Let all others keep silent a moment.
I have this word to bring,
This thing to say,
This song to sing:

Bitter was the day
When I bowed my back
Beneath the slaver's whip.

That day is past.

Bitter was the day
When I saw my children unschooled,
My young men without a voice in the world,

My women taken as the body-toys
Of a thieving people.

That day is past.

Bitter was the day, I say,
When the lyncher's rope
Hung about my neck,
And the fire scorched my feet,
And the oppressors had no pity,
And only in the sorrow songs
Relief was found.

That day is past.

I know full well now
Only my own hands,
Dark as the earth,
Can make my earth-dark body free.
O, thieves, exploiters, killers,
No longer shall you say
With arrogant eyes and scornful lips:
"You are my servant,
Black man—
I, the free!"

That day is past—

For now,
In many mouths—
Dark mouths where red tongues burn
And white teeth gleam—
New words are formed,
Bitter
With the past
But sweet
With the dream.

Tense,
Unyielding,
Strong and sure,
They sweep the earth—

Revolt! Arise!

The Black
And White World
Shall be one!
The Worker's World!

The past is done!

A new dream flames
Against the
Sun!

Sister Johnson Marches

Here am I with my head held high!
What's de matter, honey?
I just want to cry:
It's de first of May!

Here I go with my banner in my hand!
What's de matter, chile?
Why we owns de land!
It's de first of May!

Who are all them people
Marching in a mass?
Lawd! Don't you know?
That's de working class!

It's de first of May!

Open Letter to the South

White workers of the South
   Miners,
   Farmers,
   Mechanics,
   Mill hands,
   Shop girls,
   Railway men,
   Servants,
   Tobacco workers,
   Sharecroppers,
   GREETINGS!

I am the black worker,
   Listen:
That the land might be ours,
And the mines and the factories and the office towers
At Harlan, Richmond, Gastonia, Atlanta, New Orleans;
That the plants and the roads and the tools of power
Be ours:

Let us forget what Booker T. said,
"Separate as the fingers."

Let us become instead, you and I,
One single hand
That can united rise
To smash the old dead dogmas of the past—
To kill the lies of color
That keep the rich enthroned
And drive us to the time-clock and the plow
Helpless, stupid, scattered, and alone—as now—
Race against race,
Because one is black,
Another white of face.

Let us new lessons learn,
All workers,
New life-ways make,
One union form:
Until the future burns out
Every past mistake
Let us together, say:
"You are my brother, black or white,
You my sister—now—today!"
For me, no more, the great migration to the North.
Instead: migration into force and power—
Tuskegee with a new flag on the tower!
On every lynching tree, a poster crying FREE
Because, O poor white workers,
You have linked your hands with me.

We did not know that we were brothers.
Now we know!
Out of that brotherhood
Let power grow!
We did not know
That we were strong.
Now we see
In union lies our strength.
Let union be
The force that breaks the time-clock,
Smashes misery,
Takes land,
Takes factories,
Takes office towers,
Takes tools and banks and mines,
Railroads, ships and dams,
Until the forces of the world
Are ours!

White worker,
Here is my hand.

Today,
We're Man to Man.

Negro Ghetto

I looked at their black faces
And this is what I saw:
The wind imprisoned in the flesh,
The sun bound down by law.
I watched them moving, moving,
Like water down the street,
And this is what moved in my heart:
Their far-too-humble feet.

Lynching Song

Pull at the rope! Oh!
Pull it high!
Let the white folks live
And the black boy die,

Pull it, boys,
With a bloody cry
As the black boy spins
And the white folks die.

The white folks die?
What do you mean—
The white folks die?

That black boy's
Still body
Says:
NOT I!

Union

Not me alone—
I know now—
But all the whole oppressed
Poor world,
White and black,
Must put their hands with mine
To shake the pillars of those temples
Wherein the false gods dwell
And worn-out altars stand
Too well defended,
And the rule of greed's upheld—
That must be ended.

Uncollected Poems

1921–1930

Question

When the old junk man Death
Comes to gather up our bodies
And toss them into the sack of oblivion,
I wonder if he will find
The corpse of a white multi-millionaire
Worth more pennies of eternity,
Than the black torso of
A Negro cotton-picker?

My Loves

I love to see the big white moon,
   A-shining in the sky;
I love to see the little stars,
    When the shadow clouds go by.

I love the rain drops falling
   On my roof-top in the night;
I love the soft wind's sighing,
    Before the dawn's gray light.

I love the deepness of the blue,
   In my Lord's heaven above;
But better than all these things I think,
   I love my lady love.

To a Dead Friend

The moon still sends its mellow light
   Through the purple blackness of the night;
The morning star is palely bright
    Before the dawn.

The sun still shines just as before;
The rose still grows beside my door,
      But you have gone.

The sky is blue and the robin sings;
The butterflies dance on rainbow wings
      Though I am sad.

In all the earth no joy can be;
Happiness comes no more to me,
      For you are dead.

Monotony

Today like yesterday
Tomorrow like today;
The drip, drip, drip,
   Of monotony
Is wearing my life away;
Today like yesterday,
Tomorrow like today.

Dreams

Hold fast to dreams
For if dreams die
Life is a broken-winged bird
That cannot fly.

Hold fast to dreams
For when dreams go
Life is a barren field
Frozen with snow.

The Last Feast of Belshazzar

The jeweled entrails of pomegranates
    bled on the marble floor.
The jewel-heart of a virgin broke at the
    golden door.
The laughter of a drunken lord hid the sob
    of a silken whore.

Mene,
Wrote a strange hand,
Mene Tekel Upharsin,—
And Death stood at the door.

Shadows

We run,
We run,
We cannot stand these shadows!
Give us the sun.

We were not made
For shade,
For heavy shade,
And narrow space of stifling air
That these white things have made.
We run,
Oh, God,
We run!
We must break through these shadows,
We must find the sun.

My Beloved

Shall I make a record of your beauty?
Shall I write words about you?
Shall I make a poem that will live a thousand
    years and paint you in the poem?

Gods

The ivory gods,
And the ebony gods,
And the gods of diamond and jade,
Sit silently on their temple shelves
While the people
Are afraid.
Yet the ivory gods,
And the ebony gods,
And the gods of diamond-jade,
Are only silly puppet gods
That the people themselves
Have made.

Grant Park

The haunting face of poverty,
The hands of pain,
The rough, gargantuan feet of fate,
The nails of conscience in a soul
That didn't want to do wrong—
You can see what they've done
To brothers of mine
In one back-yard of Fifth Avenue.
You can see what they've done

To brothers of mine—
Sleepers on iron benches
Behind the Library in Grant Park.

Fire-Caught

The gold moth did not love him
So, gorgeous, she flew away.
But the gray moth circled the flame
   Until the break of day.
And then, with wings like a dead desire,
She fell, fire-caught, into the flame.

Prayer for a Winter Night

O, Great God of Cold and Winter,
Wrap the earth in an icy blanket
And freeze the poor in their beds.
All those who haven't enough cover
To keep them warm,
Nor food enough to keep them strong—
Freeze, dear God.
Let their limbs grow stiff
And their hearts cease to beat,
Then tomorrow
They'll wake up in some rich kingdom of nowhere
Where nothingness is everything and
Everything is nothingness.

Fascination

Her teeth are as white as the meat of an apple,
Her lips are like dark ripe plums.
I love her.
Her hair is a midnight mass, a dusky aurora.
I love her.
And because her skin is the brown of an oak leaf in autumn, but a
    softer color,
I want to kiss her.

Subway Face

That I have been looking
For you all my life
Does not matter to you.
You do not know.

You never knew.
Nor did I.
Now you take the Harlem train uptown;
I take a local down.

A Song to a Negro Wash-woman

Oh, wash-woman,
    Arms elbow-deep in white suds,
    Soul washed clean,
    Clothes washed clean,—
    I have many songs to sing you
    Could I but find the words.

Was it four o'clock or six o'clock on a winter afternoon, I saw you
  wringing out the last shirt in Miss White Lady's kitchen? Was it four
  o'clock or six o'clock? I don't remember.

But I know, at seven one spring morning you were on Vermont Street
  with a bundle in your arms going to wash clothes.
And I know I've seen you in a New York subway train in the late
  afternoon coming home from washing clothes.

Yes, I know you, wash-woman.
I know how you send your children to school, and high-school, and
  even college.
I know how you work and help your man when times are hard.
I know how you build your house up from the wash-tub and call it
  home.
And how you raise your churches from white suds for the service of the
  Holy God.

And I've seen you singing, wash-woman. Out in the back-yard garden
  under the apple trees, singing, hanging white clothes on long lines in
  the sun-shine.
And I've seen you in church a Sunday morning singing, praising your
  Jesus, because some day you're going to sit on the right hand of the
  Son of God and forget you ever were a wash-woman. And the aching
  back and the bundles of clothes will be unremembered then.
Yes, I've seen you singing.

And for you,
    O singing wash-woman,
    For you, singing little brown woman,
    Singing strong black woman,
    Singing tall yellow woman,
    Arms deep in white suds,
    Soul clean,
    Clothes clean,—

For you I have many songs to make
Could I but find the words.

Johannesburg Mines

In the Johannesburg mines
There are 240,000
Native Africans working.
What kind of poem
Would you
Make out of that?
240,000 natives
Working in the
Johannesburg mines.

To Certain Intellectuals

You are no friend of mine
For I am poor,
Black,
Ignorant and slow,—
Not your kind.
You yourself
Have told me so,—
No friend of mine.

Steel Mills

The mills
That grind and grind,
That grind out new steel
And grind away the lives

Of men,—
In the sunset
Their stacks
Are great black silhouettes
Against the sky.
In the dawn
They belch red fire.
The mills,—
Grinding out new steel,
Old men.

Liars

It is we who are liars:
The Pretenders-to-be who are not
And the Pretenders-not-to-be who are.
It is we who use words
As screens for thoughts
And weave dark garments
To cover the naked body
Of the too white Truth.
It is we with the civilized souls
    Who are liars.

Song

Lovely, dark, and lonely one,
Bare your bosom to the sun.
Do not be afraid of light,
You who are a child of night.

Open wide your arms to life,
Whirl in the wind of pain and strife,

Face the wall with the dark closed gate,
Beat with bare, brown fists—
And wait.

Walkers with the Dawn

Being walkers with the dawn and morning,
Walkers with the sun and morning,
We are not afraid of night,
Nor days of gloom,
Nor darkness—
Being walkers with the sun and morning.

Drama for Winter Night (Fifth Avenue)

You can't sleep here,
My good man,
You can't sleep here.
This is the house of God.

The usher opens the church door and he goes out.

You can't sleep in this car, old top,
Not here.
If Jones found you
He'd give you to the cops.
Get-the-hell out now,
This ain't home.
You can't stay here.

The chauffeur opens the door and he gets out.

Lord! You can't let a man lie
In the streets like this.

Find an officer quick.
Send for an ambulance.
Maybe he is sick but
He can't die on this corner,
Not here!
He can't die here.

Death opens a door.

Oh, God,
Lemme git by St. Peter.
Lemme sit down on the steps of your throne.
Lemme rest somewhere.
What did yuh say, God?
What did yuh say?
You can't sleep here. . . .
Bums can't stay. . . .

The man's raving.
Get him to the hospital quick.
He's attracting a crowd.
He can't die on this corner.
No, no, not here.

God to Hungry Child

Hungry child,
I didn't make this world for you.
You didn't buy any stock in my railroad.
You didn't invest in my corporation.
Where are your shares in standard oil?
I made the world for the rich
And the will-be-rich
And the have-always-been-rich.

Not for you,
Hungry child.

Rising Waters

To you
Who are the
Foam on the sea
And not the sea—
What of the jagged rocks,
And the waves themselves,
And the force of the mounting waters?
You are
But foam on the sea,
You rich ones—
Not the sea.

Poem to a Dead Soldier

"Death is a whore who consorts with all men."

Ice-cold passion
And a bitter breath
Adorned the bed
Of Youth and Death—
Youth, the young soldier
Who went to the wars
And embraced white Death,
the vilest of whores.

Now we spread roses
Over your tomb—
We who sent you
To your doom.

Now we make soft speeches
And sob soft cries
And throw soft flowers
And utter soft lies.

We would mould you in metal
And carve you in stone,
Not daring to make statue
Of your dead flesh and bone,
Not daring to mention
The bitter breath
Nor the ice-cold passion
Of your love-night with Death.

We make soft speeches.
We sob soft cries
We throw soft flowers,
And utter soft lies.
And you who were young
When you went to the wars
Have lost your youth now
With the vilest of whores.

Park Benching

I've sat on the park benches in Paris
Hungry.
I've sat on the park benches in New York
Hungry.
And I've said:
I want a job.
I want work.
And I've been told:
There are no jobs.

There is no work.
So I've sat on the park benches
Hungry.
Mid-winter,
Hungry days,
No jobs,
No work.

Empty House

It was in the empty house
That I came to dwell
And in the empty house
I found an empty hell.

Why is it that an empty house,
Untouched by human strife,
Can hold more woe
Than the wide world holds,
More pain than a cutting knife?

Ways

A slash of the wrist,
A swallow of scalding acid,
The crash of a bullet through the brain—
And Death comes like a mother
To hold you in her arms.

America

Little dark baby,
Little Jew baby,
Little outcast,
America is seeking the stars,
America is seeking tomorrow.
You are America.
I am America
America—the dream,
America—the vision.
America—the star-seeking I.
Out of yesterday
The chains of slavery;
Out of yesterday,
The ghettos of Europe;
Out of yesterday,
The poverty and pain of the old, old, world,
The building and struggle of this new one,
We come
You and I,
Seeking the stars.
You and I,
You of the blue eyes
And the blond hair,
I of the dark eyes
And the crinkly hair.
You and I
Offering hands
Being brothers,
Being one,
Being America.
You and I.
And I?
Who am I?

You know me:
I am Crispus Attucks at the Boston Tea Party;
Jimmy Jones in the ranks of the last black troops marching for
    democracy.
I am Sojourner Truth preaching and praying for the goodness of
    this wide, wide land;
Today's black mother bearing tomorrow's America.
Who am I?
You know me,
Dream of my dreams,
I am America.
I am America seeking the stars.
America—
Hoping, praying
Fighting, dreaming.
Knowing
There are stains
On the beauty of my democracy,
I want to be clean.
I want to grovel
No longer in the mire.
I want to reach always
After stars.
Who am I?
I am the ghetto child,
I am the dark baby,
I am you
And the blond tomorrow
And yet
I am my one sole self,
America seeking the stars.

Better

Better in the quiet night
To sit and cry alone
Than rest my head on another's shoulder
After you have gone.

Better, in the brilliant day,
Filled with sun and noise,
To listen to no song at all
Than hear another voice.

Change

The moon is fat and old tonight,
Yellow and gross with pain.
The moon is fat and old tonight,
But she'll be young again.
Whereas my love, who's fair and sweet,
My love, who's sweet and fair,
Will wither like the autumn rose
In winter air.

Poem (When Young Spring Comes)

When young spring comes,
With silver rain
One almost
Could be good again.

But then comes summer,
Whir of bees . . .
Crimson poppies . . . anemones,

The old, old god of Love
To please.

Love Song for Antonia

If I should sing
All of my songs for you
And you would not listen to them,
If I should build
All of my dream houses for you
And you would never live in them,
If I should give
All of my hopes to you
And you would laugh and say: I do not care,
Still I would give you my love
Which is more than my songs,
More than any houses of dreams,
Or dreams of houses—
I would still give you my love
Though you never looked at me.

A Wooing

I will bring you big things:
Colors of dawn-morning,
Beauty of rose leaves,
And a flaming love.

But you say
Those are not big things,
That only money counts.

Well,
Then I will bring you money.
But do not ask me
For the beauty of rose leaves,
Nor the colors of dawn-morning,
Nor a flaming love.

To Certain "Brothers"

You sicken me with lies,
With truthful lies.
And with your pious faces.
And your wide, out-stretched,
    mock-welcome, Christian hands.
While underneath
Is dirt and ugliness,
And rottening hearts,
And wild hyenas howling
In your soul's waste lands.

Minstrel Man

Because my mouth
Is wide with laughter
And my throat
Is deep with song,
You do not think
I suffer after
I have held my pain
So long?

Because my mouth
Is wide with laughter,

You do not hear
My inner cry?
Because my feet
Are gay with dancing,
You do not know
I die?

Fog

Singing black boatmen
An August morning
In the thick white fog at Sekondi
Coming out to take cargo
From anchored alien ships,
You do not know the fog
We strange so-civilized ones
Sail in always.

Star Seeker

I have been a seeker
Seeking a flaming star,
And the flame white star
Has burned my hands
Even from afar.

Walking in a dream-dead world
Circled by iron bars,
I sought a singing star's
Wild beauty.
Now behold my scars.

Lullaby (For a Black Mother)

My little dark baby,
My little earth-thing,
My little love-one,
What shall I sing
For your lullaby?

    Stars,
    Stars,
    A necklace of stars
    Winding the night.

My little black baby,
My dark body's baby,
What shall I sing
For your lullaby?

    Moon,
    Moon,
    Great diamond moon,
    Kissing the night.

Oh, little dark baby,
Night black baby,

    Stars, stars,
    Moon,
    Night stars,
    Moon,

For your sleep-song lullaby.

The Ring

Love is the master of the ring
And life a circus tent.
What is this silly song you sing?
Love is the master of the ring.

I am afraid!
Afraid of Love
And of Love's bitter whip!
Afraid,
Afraid of Love
And Love's sharp, stinging whip.

What is this silly song you sing?
Love is the master of the ring.

Teacher

Ideals are like the stars,
    Always above our reach.
Humbly I tried to learn,
    More humbly did I teach.

On all honest virtues
    I sought to keep firm hold.
I wanted to be a good man
    Though I pinched my soul.

But now I lie beneath cool loam
    Forgetting every dream;
And in this narrow bed of earth
    No lights gleam.

In this narrow bed of earth
   Star-dust never scatters,
And I tremble lest the darkness teach
   Me that nothing matters.

Love Song for Lucinda

Love
Is a ripe plum
Growing on a purple tree.
Taste it once
And the spell of its enchantment
Will never let you be.

Love
Is a bright star
Glowing in far Southern skies.
Look too hard
And its burning flame
Will always hurt your eyes.

Love
Is a high mountain
Stark in a windy sky.
If you
Would never lose your breath.
Do not climb too high.

Fortune Teller Blues

I went to de gypsy,
De gypsy took hold o' my hand.
Went to de gypsy,

Gypsy took hold o' my hand.
She looked at me and tole me
Chile, you gonna lose yo' man.

These fortune tellers
Never tell me nothin' kind.
I say fortune tellers
Never tell me nothin' kind.
I'd give a hundred dollars
To de one that would ease my mind.

Cause I'll holler an' scream an'
Fall down on de flo'.
Say I'll holler an' scream an'
Fall down on de flo'.
If my man leaves me
I won't live no mo'.

Wide River

Ma baby lives across de river
An' I ain't got no boat.
She lives across de river.
I ain't got no boat.
I ain't a good swimmer
An' I don't know how to float.

Wide, wide river
'Twixt ma love an' me.
Wide, wide river
'Twixt ma love an' me.
I never knowed how
Wide a river can be.

Got to cross that river
An' git to ma baby somehow.
Cross that river,
Git to ma baby somehow—
Cause if I don't see ma baby
I'll lay down an' die right now.

Pale Lady

Pale, delightful lady,
How I love you!
I would spread cool violets
At your feet
And bring you lovely jewels
For your hair,
And put a tiny golden ring
Upon your finger
And leave it there
As a sign and symbol of my love,
My bright, bright love for you.
Oh, pale, delightful lady,
How I love you!

New Year

The years
Fall like dry leaves
From the top-less tree
Of eternity.
Does it matter
That another leaf has fallen?

Epitaph

Within this grave lie,
Yes, I.
Why laugh, good people,
Or why cry?
Within this grave
Lies nothing more
Than I.

Autumn Note

The little flowers of yesterday
Have all forgotten May.
The last gold leaf
Has turned to brown.
The last bright day is grey.
The cold of winter comes apace
And you have gone away.

Formula

Poetry should treat
    Of lofty things
Soaring thoughts
    And birds with wings.

The Muse of Poetry
    Should not know
That roses
    In manure grow.

The Muse of Poetry
    Should not care
That earthly pain
    Is everywhere.

Poetry!
    Treats of lofty things:
Soaring thoughts
    And birds with wings.

To Beauty

To worship
At the altar of Beauty,
To feel her loveliness and pain,
To thrill
At the wonder of her gorgeous moon
Or the sharp, swift, silver swords
Of falling rain.

To walk in a golden garden
When an autumn sun
Has almost set,
When near-night's purple splendor
Shimmers to a star-shine net.
To worship
At the altar of Beauty
Is a pleasure divine,
Not given to the many many
But to fools
Who drink Beauty's wine.
Not given to the many many
But to fools
Who seek no other goddess

Nor grapes
Plucked from another's
Vine.

Lonesome Place

I got to leave this town.
It's a lonesome place.
Got to leave this town cause
It's a lonesome place.
A po', po' boy can't
Find a friendly face.

Goin' down to de river
Flowin' deep an' slow.
Goin' down to de river
Deep an' slow,—
Cause there ain't no worries
Where de waters go.

I'm weary, weary,
Weary as I can be.
Weary, weary,
Weary as can be.
This life's so weary,
'S 'bout to overcome me.

Pictures to the Wall

Shall I tell you of my old, old dreams
Lost at the earth's strange turnings,
Some in the sea when the waves foamed high,
Some in a garret candle's burnings?

Shall I tell you of bitter, forgotten dreams—
You who are still so young, so young?
You with your wide brown singing eyes
And laughter at the tip of your tongue.

Shall I tell you of weary, weary dreams,—
You who have lost no dreams at all,
Or shall I keep quiet and let turn
My ugly pictures to the wall?

Red Roses

I'm waitin' for de springtime
When de tulips grow—
Sweet, sweet springtime
When de tulips grow;
Cause if I'd die in de winter
They'd bury me under snow.

Un'neath de snow, Lawd,
Oh, what would I do?
Un'neath de snow,
I say what would I do?
It's bad enough to die but
I don't want freezin' too.

I'm waitin' for de springtime
An' de roses red,
Waitin' for de springtime
When de roses red
'Ll make a nice coverin'
Fer a gal that's dead.

Argument

Now lookahere, gal,
Don't you talk 'bout me.
I got mo' hair 'n you evah did see,
An' if I ain't high yaller
I ain't coal black,
So what you said 'bout me
You bettah take it back.

   Now, listen, Corrine,
   I don't talk 'bout you.
   I's got much mo'
   Important things to do.

All right, gal,
But I'm speakin' ma mind:
You bettah keep yo' freight train
Off ma line.

A Letter to Anne

Since I left you, Anne,
I have seen nothing but you.
Every day
Has been your face,
And every night your hand
And every road
Your voice calling me.
And every rock and every flower and tree
Has been a touch of you.
Nowhere
Have I seen anything else but you,
Anne.

In the Mist of the Moon

In the mist of the moon I saw you,
O, Nanette,
And you were lovelier than the moon.
   You were darkness,
   And the body of darkness.
   And light,
   And the body of light.
In the mist of the moon I saw you,
Dark Nanette.

For an Indian Screen

Clutching at trees and clawing rocks
And panting and climbing
Until he reached the top
A tiger in India
Surmounted a cliff one day
When the hunters were behind him
And his lair was far away.
A black and golden tiger
Climbed a red cliff's side
And men in black and golden gowns
Sought the tiger's hide.

O, splendid, supple animal:
Against the cliff's red face:
A picture for an Indian screen
Woven in silks of subtle sheen
And broidered in yellow lace,
A picture for an Indian screen
As a prince's gift to some ebony queen
In a far-off land like a fairy scene.

Day

Where most surely comes a day
When all the sweets you've gorged
Will turn your stomach sick
And all the friends you've loved
Will go away
And every gold swift hour
Will be an hour of pain
And every sun-filled cloud
A cloud of rain
And even the withered flowers
Will lose their long-held faint perfume
And you alone will be with you
In that last room,—
Only your single selves together
Facing a single doom.

Passing Love

Because you are to me a song
I must not sing you over-long.

Because you are to me a prayer
I cannot say you everywhere.

Because you are to me a rose—
You will not stay when summer goes.

Lincoln Monument: Washington

Let's go see old Abe
Sitting in the marble and the moonlight,
Sitting lonely in the marble and the moonlight,
Quiet for ten thousand centuries, old Abe.
Quiet for a million, million years.

Quiet—

And yet a voice forever
Against the
Timeless walls
Of time—
Old Abe.

Bulwark

You were the last bulwark of my dreams,
And now you, too, have tumbled down into the dust.
You, too, are no more than a broken lie.
   Something
   came between us
   green and slimy
   like sickly laughter
   and a bowl was broken
   from which
   we could not drink thereafter
   and we turned around
   and threw
   the scattered bits
   upon the ground
   and went our separate ways
   into the town
   and a clock

somewhere in a tower
boomed out slowly
hour after hour
a great cracked
broken sound.
You were the last bulwark of my dreams,
And now you, too, have tumbled down.

Poem for Youth

Raindrops
On the crumbling walls
Of tradition,
Sunlight
Across mouldy pits
Of yesterday.

Oh,
Wise old men,
What do you say
About the fiddles
And the jazz
And the loud Hey! Hey!
About the dancing girls,
And the laughing boys,
And the brilliant lights,
And the blaring joys,
The firecracker days
And the nights,—
Love-toys?

Staid old men,
What do you say
About sun-filled rain
Drowning yesterday?

The Naughty Child

The naughty child
Who ventured to go cut flowers,
Fell into the mill-pond
And was drowned.
But the good children all
Are living yet,
Nice folks now
In a very nice town.

Wise Men

Let me become dead eyed
Like a fish,—
I'm sure then I'd be wise
For all the wise men I've seen
Have had dead eyes.

Let me learn to fit all things
Into law and rule:
I'd be the proper person then
To teach a school.

Ma Lord

Ma Lord ain't no stuck-up man.
Ma Lord, he ain't proud.
When he goes a-walkin'
He gives me his hand.
"You ma friend," he 'lowed.

Ma Lord knowed what it was to work.
He knowed how to pray.
Ma Lord's life was trouble, too,
Trouble ever day.

Ma Lord ain't no stuck-up man.
He's a friend o' mine.
When He went to heaben,
His soul on fire,
He tole me I was gwine.
He said, "Sho you'll come wid Me
An' be ma friend through eternity."

Tapestry

Men who ride strange wild horses
Down dangerous glens and glades,
Men who draw keen sharp swords,
Toledo or Damascus blades,
Men who swear and laugh and love
And live and sing like troubadours,—
Wrinkled old beldams somewhere
Are dreaming of old amours.

Success

Here I sit with my belly full
And he who might have been my brother
Walks hungry in the rain.

Here I sit with my belly full
And she I might have loved
Seeks someone in the shadows
To whom she may sell her body.

Here I sit with my belly full,
No longer in the rain,
No longer the shadows for the
Woman I love,
No longer hunger.

Success is a great big beefsteak
With onions on it,
And I eat.

Nocturne for the Drums

Gay little devils
That hide in gin
And tickle black boys
Under the chin
And make them laugh,
Gay little devils
That lurk in kisses,
And shine in the eyes
Of ebony misses,
Shine in their eyes:
Whee-e-e!!
O-o-o-o . . . Boom!
Jazz band in a cabaret!
The quick red hour
Before the day.

For Salome

There
Is no sweetness
In the kiss

Of a mouth
Unwarm and dead,
And even passion's
Flaming bliss
Turns ashen
In a charnel bed.
Salome
Of the wine-red lips,
What would you with death's head?

Being Old

It's because you are so young,—
You do not understand.
   But we are old
   As the jungle trees
   That bloomed forever,
   Old as the forgotten rivers
   That flowed into the earth.
Surely we know what you do not know;
   Joy of living,
   Uselessness of things.
You are too young to understand yet.
   Build another skyscraper
   Touching the stars.
We sit with our backs against a tree
And watch skyscrapers tumble
And stars forget.
   Solomon built a temple
   And it must have fallen down.
   It isn't here now.
We know some things, being old,
You do not understand.

Freedom Seeker

I see a woman with wings
Trying to escape from a cage
And the cage door
Has fallen on her wings.
They are long wings
Which drag on the ground
When she stands up,
But she hasn't enough strength
To pull them away
From the weight of the cage door,
She is caught and held by her wings.

Parisian Beggar Woman

Once you were young.
Now, hunched in the cold,
Nobody cares
That you are old.

Once you were beautiful.
Now, in the street,
No one remembers
Your lips were sweet.

Oh, withered old woman
Of rue Fontaine,
Nobody but death
Will kiss you again.

I Thought It Was Tangiers I Wanted

I know now
That Notre Dame is in Paris.
And the Seine is more to me now
Than a wriggling line on a map
Or a name in travel stories.

I know now
There is a Crystal Palace in Antwerp
Where a hundred women sell their naked bodies,
And the night-lovers of sailors
Wait for men on docks in Genoa.

I know now
That a great golden moon
Like a picture-book moon
Really rises behind palm groves
In Africa,
And tom-toms do beat
In village squares under the mango trees.

I know now
That Venice is a church dome
And a net-work of canals,
Tangiers a whiteness under sun.
I thought
It was Tangiers I wanted,
Or the gargoyles of Notre Dame,
Or the Crystal Palace in Antwerp,
Or the golden palm-grove moon in Africa,
Or a church dome and a net-work of canals.

Happiness lies nowhere,
Some old fool said,
If not within oneself.

It's a sure thing
Notre Dame is in Paris,—
But I thought it was Tangiers I wanted.

Dreamer

I take my dreams
And make of them a bronze vase,
And a wide round fountain
With a beautiful statue in its center,
And a song with a broken heart,
And I ask you:
Do you understand my dreams?
Sometimes you say you do
And sometimes you say you don't.
Either way
It doesn't matter.
I continue to dream.

Sunset—Coney Island

The sun,
Like the red yolk of a rotten egg,
Falls behind the roller-coaster
And the horizon sticks
With a putrid odor of colors.
Down on the beach
A little Jewish tailor from the Bronx,
With a bad stomach,
Throws up the hot-dog sandwiches
He ate in the afternoon
While life to him
Is like a sick tomato
In a garbage can.

Lover's Return

My old time daddy
Came back home last night.
His face was pale and
His eyes didn't look just right.

He says, "Mary, I'm
Comin' home to you—
So sick and lonesome
I don't know what to do."

    Oh, men treats women
    Just like a pair o' shoes—
    You kicks 'em round and
    Does 'em like you choose.

I looked at my daddy—
Lawd! and I wanted to cry.
He looked so thin—
Lawd! that I wanted to cry.
But the devil told me:
    Damn a lover
    Come home to die!

Nonette

You wound my soul with a thousand spears,
You bathe my wounds in a flood of tears,
Nonette.

You give me a rose whose breath is sweet,
Whose petals are poison and death to eat,
Nonette.

And when I am dead you do not cry,
But your poor heart breaks, too, and you, too, die.

Alabama Earth

(At Booker Washington's grave)

Deep in Alabama earth
His buried body lies—
But higher than the singing pines
And taller than the skies
And out of Alabama earth
To all the world there goes
The truth a simple heart has held
And the strength a strong hand knows,
While over Alabama earth
These words are gently spoken:
Serve—and hate will die unborn.
Love—and chains are broken.

Hurt

Who cares
About the hurt in your heart?

Make a song like this
    for a jazz band to play:

    Nobody cares.
    Nobody cares.

Make a song like that
From your lips.

    Nobody cares.

Lady in Cabaret

She knows
The end of the evening will come,—
It has come before.
And if it should never come again.
Well,—
Just that much more
A bore.

Old Youth

I heard a child's voice,
Strong, clear, and full of youth,
But I looked into his face
And the face was old,—
Not old with age,
But old with city knowledge,
Old with work
And the dust and grime
Of the factories.
O little child's voice,
O face like a flowerless spring!

Anne Spencer's Table

On Anne Spencer's table
There lies an unsharpened pencil—
As though she has left unwritten
Many things she knows to write.

Spring for Lovers

Desire weaves its fantasy of dreams,
And all the world becomes a garden close
In which we wander, you and I together,
Believing in the symbol of the rose,
Believing only in the heart's bright flower—
Forgetting—flowers wither in an hour.

The English

In ships all over the world
The English comb their hair for dinner,
Stand watch on the bridge,
Guide by strange stars,
Take on passengers,
Slip up hot rivers,
Nose across lagoons,
Bargain for trade,
Buy, sell or rob,
Load oil, load fruit,
Load cocoa beans, load gold
In ships all over the world,
Comb their hair for dinner.

Rent-Party Shout: For a Lady Dancer

Whip it to a jelly!
Too bad Jim!
Mamie's got ma man—
An' I can't find him.
Shake that thing! O!
Shake it slow!

That man I love is
Mean an' low.
Pistol an' razor!
Razor an' gun!
If I sees ma man he'd
Better run—
For I'll shoot him in de shoulder,
Else I'll cut him down,
Cause I knows I can find him
When he's in de ground—
Then can't no other women
Have him layin' round.
So play it, Mr. Nappy!
Yo' music's fine!
I'm gonna kill that
Man o' mine!

Black Seed

World-wide dusk
Of dear dark faces
Driven before an alien wind,
Scattered like seed
From far-off places
Growing in soil
That's strange and thin,
Hybrid plants
In another's garden,
Flowers
In a land
That's not your own,
Cut by the shears
Of the white-faced gardeners—

Tell them to leave you alone!

Merry Christmas

Merry Christmas, China,
From the gun-boats in the river,
Ten-inch shells for Christmas gifts,
And peace on earth forever.

Merry Christmas, India,
To Gandhi in his cell,
From righteous Christian England,
Ring out, bright Christmas bell!

Ring Merry Christmas, Africa,
From Cairo to the Cape!
Ring Hallehuiah! Praise the Lord!
(For murder and for rape.)

Ring Merry Christmas, Haiti!
(And drown the voodoo drums—
We'll rob you to the Christian hymns
Until the next Christ comes.)

Ring Merry Christmas, Cuba!
(While Yankee domination
Keeps a nice fat president
In a little half-starved nation.)

And to you down-and-outers,
("Due to economic laws")
Oh, eat, drink, and be merry
With a bread-line Santa Claus—

While all the world hails Christmas,
While all the church bells sway!
While, better still, the Christian guns
Proclaim this joyous day!

While holy steel that makes us strong
Spits forth a mighty Yuletide song:
SHOOT Merry Christmas everywhere!
Let Merry Christmas GAS the air!

Uncollected Poems

1931–1940

Tired

I am so tired of waiting,
Aren't you,
For the world to become good
And beautiful and kind?
Let us take a knife
And cut the world in two—
And see what worms are eating
At the rind.

Call to Creation

Listen!
All you beauty-makers,
Give up beauty for a moment.
Look at harshness, look at pain,
Look at life again.
Look at hungry babies crying,
Listen to the rich men lying,
Look at starving China dying.
Hear the rumble in the East:
"In spite of all,
Life must not cease."
In India with folded arms,
In China with the guns,
In Africa with bitter smile—
See where the murmur runs:
"Life must not cease,
Because the fat and greedy ones
Proclaim their thieving peace."
Their peace far worse than war and death—
For this is better than living breath:
Free! To be Free!

Listen!
Futile beauty-makers—
Work for a while with the pattern-breakers!
Come for a march with the new-world-makers:
Let beauty be!

To Certain Negro Leaders

Voices crying in the wilderness
At so much per word
From the white folks:
"Be meek and humble,
All you niggers,
And do not cry
Too loud."

A Christian Country

God slumbers in a back alley
With a gin bottle in His hand.
Come on, God, get up and fight
Like a man.

To the Little Fort of San Lazaro
on the Ocean Front, Havana

Watch tower once for pirates
That sailed the sun-bright seas—
Red pirates, great romantics.

DRAKE
DE PLAN,
EL GRILLO

Against such as these
Years and years ago
You served quite well—
When time and ships were slow.
   But now,
Against a pirate called
THE NATIONAL CITY BANK
What can you do alone?
Would it not be
Just as well you tumbled down,
Stone by helpless stone?

House in the World

I'm looking for a house
In the world
Where the white shadows
Will not fall.

There is no such house,
Dark brothers,
No such house
At all.

Dying Beast

Sensing death,
The buzzards gather—
Noting the last struggle

Of flesh under weather,
Noting the last glance
Of agonized eye
At passing wind
And boundless sky.
Sensing death,
The buzzards overhead
Await that still moment
When life—

Is dead.

God

I am God—
Without one friend,
Alone in my purity
World without end.

Below me young lovers
Tread the sweet ground—
But I am God—
I cannot come down.

Spring!
Life is love!
Love is life only!
Better to be human
Than God—and lonely.

Scottsboro

8 BLACK BOYS IN A SOUTHERN JAIL.
  WORLD, TURN PALE!

8 black boys and one white lie.
Is it much to die?

Is it much to die when immortal feet
March with you down Time's street,
When beyond steel bars sound the deathless drums
Like a mighty heart-beat as They come?

Who comes?

Christ,
Who fought alone.

John Brown.

That mad mob
That tore the Bastille down
Stone by stone.

Moses.

Jeanne d'Arc.

Dessalines.

Nat Turner.

Fighters for the free.

Lenin with the flag blood red.

(Not dead! Not dead!
None of those is dead.)

Gandhi.

Sandino.

Evangelista, too,
To walk with you—

8 BLACK BOYS IN A SOUTHERN JAIL.
WORLD, TURN PALE!

Advertisement for the Waldorf-Astoria

Fine living . . . à la carte??
Come to the Waldorf-Astoria!

    LISTEN, HUNGRY ONES!
Look! See what *Vanity Fair* says about the
    new Waldorf-Astoria:
      "All the luxuries of private home. . . ."
Now, won't that be charming when the last flop-house has turned you
    down this winter?
    Furthermore:
"It is far beyond anything hitherto attempted in the hotel world. . . ."
    It cost twenty-eight million dollars. The famous Oscar Tschirky is in
    charge of banqueting. Alexandre Gastaud is chef. It will be a
    distinguished background for society.
So when you've got no place else to go, homeless and hungry ones,
    choose the Waldorf as a background for your rags—
(Or do you still consider the subway after midnight good enough?)

          ROOMERS
Take a room at the new Waldorf, you down-and-outers—sleepers in
    charity's flop-houses where God pulls a long face, and you have to
    pray to get a bed.
They serve swell board at the Waldorf-Astoria. Look at this menu, will
    you:

GUMBO CREOLE
CRABMEAT IN CASSOLETTE
BOILED BRISKET OF BEEF
SMALL ONIONS IN CREAM
WATERCRESS SALAD
PEACH MELBA

Have luncheon there this afternoon, all you jobless.
  Why not?
Dine with some of the men and women who got rich off of your labor,
  who clip coupons with clean white fingers because your hands dug
  coal, drilled stone, sewed garments, poured steel to let other people
  draw dividends and live easy.
(Or haven't you had enough yet of the soup-lines and the bitter bread
  of charity?)
Walk through Peacock Alley tonight before dinner, and get warm,
  anyway. You've got nothing else to do.

EVICTED FAMILIES
All you families put out in the street:
  Apartments in the Towers are only $10,000 a year.
    (Three rooms and two baths.) Move in there until times get good,
    and you can do better. $10,000 and $1.00 are about the same to
    you, aren't they?
Who cares about money with a wife and kids homeless, and nobody in
  the family working? Wouldn't a duplex high above the street be
  grand, with a view of the richest city in the world at your nose?
"A lease, if you prefer, or an arrangement terminable at will."

NEGROES
Oh, Lawd, I done forgot Harlem!
Say, you colored folks, hungry a long time in 135th Street—they got
  swell music at the Waldorf-Astoria. It sure is a mighty nice place to
  shake hips in, too. There's dancing after supper in a big warm room.
  It's cold as hell on Lenox Avenue. All you've had all day is a cup of
  coffee. Your pawnshop overcoat's a ragged banner on your hungry

frame. You know, downtown folks are just crazy about Paul
Robeson! Maybe they'll like you, too, black mob from Harlem.
Drop in at the Waldorf this afternoon for tea. Stay to dinner. Give
Park Avenue a lot of darkie color—free for nothing! Ask the Junior
Leaguers to sing a spiritual for you. They probably know 'em better
than you do—and their lips won't be so chapped with cold after they
step out of their closed cars in the undercover driveways.
>   *Hallelujah! Undercover driveways!*
>   *Ma soul's a witness for de Waldorf-Astoria!*
(A thousand nigger section-hands keep the roadbeds smooth, so
    investments in railroads pay ladies with diamond necklaces staring at
    Sert murals.)
>   *Thank God A-mighty!*
(And a million niggers bend their backs on rubber plantations, for rich
    behinds to ride on thick tires to the Theatre Guild tonight.)
>   *Ma soul's a witness!*
(And here we stand, shivering in the cold, in Harlem.)
>   *Glory be to God—*
>   *De Waldorf-Astoria's open!*

EVERYBODY

So get proud and rare back; everybody! The new Waldorf-Astoria's
    open!
(Special siding for private cars from the railroad yards.)
    You ain't been there yet?
(A thousand miles of carpet and a million bathrooms.)
    What's the matter?
You haven't seen the ads in the papers? Didn't you get a card? Don't
    you know they specialize in American cooking? Ankle on down to
    49th Street at Park Avenue. Get up off that subway bench tonight
    with the evening POST for cover! Come on out o' that flop-house!
    Stop shivering your guts out all day on street corners under the El.
Jesus, ain't you tired yet?

CHRISTMAS CARD

Hail Mary, Mother of God!
  the new Christ child of the Revolution's about to be born.
(Kick hard, red baby, in the bitter womb of the mob.)
Somebody, put an ad in *Vanity Fair* quick!
Call Oscar of the Waldorf—for Christ's sake!! It's almost Christmas,
  and that little girl—turned whore because her belly was too hungry
  to stand it anymore—wants a nice clean bed for the Immaculate
  Conception.
Listen, Mary, Mother of God, wrap your new born babe in the red flag
  of Revolution: the Waldorf-Astoria's the best manger we've got. For
  reservations: Telephone EL. 5–3000.

Helen Keller

She,
In the dark,
Found light
Brighter than many ever see.
She,
Within herself,
Found loveliness,
Through the soul's own mastery.
And now the world receives
From her dower:
The message of the strength
Of inner power.

The Colored Soldier

A dramatic recitation to be done in the half-dark by a young brown fellow who has a vision of his brother killed in France while fighting for the United States of America. Martial music on a piano, or by an orchestra, may accompany the recitation—echoing softly, "Over There," "There's a Rose That Grows in No-Man's Land," "Joan of Arc," and various other war-time melodies.

THE MOOD	THE POEM
Calmly	My brother died in France—but I came back.
telling	We were just two colored boys, brown and black,
the story.	Who joined up to fight for the U.S.A.
Proudly	When the Nation called us that mighty day.
and	We were sent to training camp, then overseas—
expectantly	And me and my brother were happy as you please
with	Thinking we were fighting for Democracy's true reign
head up,	And that our dark blood would wipe away the stain
shoulders	Of prejudice, and hate, and the false color line—
back,	And give us the rights that are yours and mine.
and eyes	They told us America would know no black or white:
shining.	So we marched to the front, happy to fight.
Quietly	
recalling	Last night in a dream my brother came to me
the vision.	Out of his grave from over the sea,
The dead	Back from the acres of crosses in France,
man speaks	And said to me, "Brother, you've got your chance,
with his	And I hope you're making good, and doing fine—
face	'Cause when I was living, I didn't have mine.
full of	Black boys couldn't work then anywhere like they can
light	today,
and faith,	Could hardly find a job that offered decent pay.
confident	The unions barred us; the factories, too,
that a	But now I know we've got plenty to do.
new world	We couldn't eat in restaurants; had Jim Crow cars;
has been	Didn't have any schools; and there were all sorts of
made.	bars
Proud	To a colored boy's rising in wealth or station—
and	But now I know well that's not our situation:
smiling.	The world's been made safe for Democracy
But	And no longer do we know the dark misery—
the	Of being held back, of having no chance—
living,	Since the colored soldiers came home from France.
remembering	Didn't our government tell us things would be fine

*with a
half-sob
and
bowing
his head
in shame,
becomes
suddenly
fierce
and
angry.*

When we got through fighting, Over There, and dying?
So now I know we blacks are just like any other—
'Cause that's what I died for—isn't it, Brother?"
And I saw him standing there, straight and tall,
In his soldier's uniform, and all.
Then his dark face smiled at me in the night—
But the dream was cruel—and bitter—and somehow
    not right.
It was awful—facing that boy who went out to die,
For what could I answer him, except, "It's a lie!"

It's a lie! It's a lie! Every word they said.
And it's better a thousand times you're in France dead.
For here in the South there's no votes and no right.
And I'm still just a "nigger" in America tonight.

*Then
he sadly
recalls
the rows
of white
crosses
in France.*

Then I woke up, and the dream was ended—
But broken was the soldier's dream, too bad to be
    mended.
And it's a good thing all the black boys lying dead
    Over There
Can't see! And don't know! And won't ever care!

Broke

A complaint to be given by a dejected looking fellow shuffling along in an old suit and a battered hat, to the tune of a slow-drag stomp or a weary blues.

Uh! I sho am tired.
Been walkin' since five this mornin'.
Up and down, and they just *ain't* no jobs in this man's town.
Answerin' them want-ads not nary bit o' fun,
'Cause 'fore you gets there, ten thousand and one
Done beat you to de place, standin' outside de do'
Talkin' 'bout "we'll work for 50¢ a day, if we can't get no mo'."
And one old funny boy said, "I'll work at any price
Just only providin' de boss man is nice!"
You all out there laughin', but that ain't no joke—
When you're broke.

Last job I had, went to work at five in de mornin', or little mo'
And de man come tellin' me I better get there at fo'.
I mean four—before daylight—s'pose to've done hit yo' first stroke—
Folks sho is gettin' hard on you—just 'cause you broke.
So I say, "Mister, I ain't no sweepin' machine."
So de man say, "I'll get somebody else, then, to clean,"—
So here I is, broke.

Landlady 'lowed to me last week, "Sam, ain't you got no money?"
I say, "Now, baby, you know I ain't got none, honey."
And don't you know that old woman swelled up like a speckled toad
And told me I'd *better* pay her for my room rent and board!
After all them dollars I gived her these last two years,
And she been holdin' 'em so tight till de eagle's in tears—
I wouldn't pay her a penny now if I was to croak—
Come bawlin' me out, 'cause I'm broke.
(I don't care nothin' 'bout her myself!)

Um-mm! Sign here says they wants somebody to shovel coal.
Well, ain't never done it, but for to keep body and soul
Together, reckon I'll try . . . Sho, I wants de job! Yes, sir!
Has I did it befo'? Certainly!
What I don't know 'bout shovelin' coal, ain't no mo' to know!
Willing worker? Un-uh! Yes! What's that you say?
De time is fourteen hours a day?
Well, er—er . . . how much does you pay?
Six dollars a week? Whee-ooo! You sho pays well!
You can take that job and go to——-I hope you choke,
Even if I is broke.

But I sho been lookin' round hard lately for ways and means
O' gettin' a new winter coat, or havin' that old one cleaned.
Tried to find one o' them little elevator and switchboard jobs they used
    to have,
But they givin' 'em to school boys now and payin' just about half.
So I went down town to a hotel where I used to work at night,

And de man come tellin' me they ain't hirin' no mo' colored—just
  white.
I can't even get de money for to buy myself a smoke,
I tell you it's awful, when you're broke.

And I sho had a pretty gal, too, up yonder on Sugar Hill.
She bought a new hat last week and come sendin' me the bill.
I said, "Baby, you know I loves you, and all like that
But right long through here now, I can't 'ford to buy you no hat."
So when I got ready to go, I said, "I'll be seein' you soon, Marie."
And she come tellin' me, she ain't got no mo' evenings free!
I thought love was a dream, but I sho have awoke—
Since I'm broke.

'Course, you hears plenty 'bout this-here unemployment relief—
But you don't see no presidents dyin' o' grief—
All this talkin' ain't nothin' but tinklin' symbols and soundin' brass:
Lawd, folkses, how much longer is this gonna last?
It's done got me so crazy, feel like I been takin' coke,
But I can't even buy a paper—I'm so broke.

Aw-oo! Yonder comes a woman I used to know way down South.
(Ain't seen her in six years! Used to go with her, too!)
She would be alright if she wasn't so bow-legged, and cross-eyed,
And didn't have such a big mouth.
Howdy-do, daughter! Caledonia, how are you?
Yes, indeedy, I sho have missed *you*, too!
All these years you say you been *workin'* here?
You got a good job? Yes! Well, I sho am glad to see *you*, dear!
Is I married? No, all these-here girls up North is too light.
Does I wanta? Well, can't say but what I might—
If a pretty gal like you was willin', I'd bite.
You still bakes biscuits? Fried chicken every night? Is that true?
Certainly, chile, I always was crazy 'bout you!
Let's get married right now! Yes! What do you say?
(Is you lookin' at me, baby, or some other way?)

'Cause I'm just dyin' to take on that there marriage yoke.
Yes, um-hum! You sho is sweet! Can you pay fo' de license, dear?
'Cause I'm broke.

The Black Clown

A dramatic monologue to be spoken by a pure-blooded Negro in the
white suit and hat of a clown, to the music of a piano, or an orchestra.

THE MOOD
A gay and
low-down blues.
Comic entrance
like the clowns
in the circus.
Humorous
defiance.
Melancholy
jazz. Then
defiance again
followed by
loud joy.
A burst of
music. Strutting
and dancing.
Then sudden
sadness again.
Back bent as
in the fields.
The slow step.
The bowed head.
"Nobody knows
de trouble I've
had."
Flinching
under the whip.
The spiritual
syncopated.
Determined to
laugh.
A bugle call.

THE POEM
You laugh
Because I'm poor and black and funny—
Not the same as you—
Because my mind is dull
And dice instead of books will do
For me to play with
When the day is through.

I am the fool of the whole world.
Laugh and push me down.
Only in song and laughter
I rise again—a black clown.
Strike up the music.
Let it be gay.
Only in joy
Can a clown have his day.

Three hundred years
In the cotton and the cane,
Plowing and reaping
With no gain—
Empty handed as I began.

A slave—under the whip,
Beaten and sore.
God! Give me laughter
That I can stand more.

God! Give me the spotted
Garments of a clown
So that the pain and the shame
Will not pull me down.

*Gay, martial
music. Walking
proudly, almost
prancing.
But gradually
subdued to a
slow, heavy
pace. "Some-
times I feel
like a mother-
less chile."
Turning futilely
from one side
to the other.
But now a harsh
and bitter note
creeps into
the music.
Over-burdened.
Backing away
angrily.
Frantic
with
humiliation
and helpless-
ness.
The music
is like
a mourn-
ful tom-tom
in the dark!
But out of
sadness
it rises to
defiance
and determina-
tion. A hymn
of faith
echoes the
fighting
"Marseillaise."*

Freedom!
Abe Lincoln done set me free—
One little moment
To dance with glee.

Then sadness again—
No land, no house, no job
No place to go.
Black—in a white world
Where cold winds blow.
The long struggle for life:
No schools, no work—
Not wanted here; not needed there—
Black—you can die.
Nobody will care—

Yet clinging to the ladder,
Round by round,
Trying to climb up,
Forever pushed down.

Day after day
White spit in my face—
Worker and clown am I
For the "civilized" race.

Nigger! Nigger! Nigger!
Scorn crushing me down.
Laugh at me! Laugh at me!
Just a black clown.

Laugh at me then,
All the world round—
From Africa to Georgia
I'm only a clown!

But no! Not forever
Like this will I be:
Here are my hands
That can really make me free!

Suffer and struggle.
Work, pray, and fight.
Smash my way through
To Manhood's true right.

Tearing off
his clown's
suit, throwing
down the hat
of a fool,
and standing
forth,
straight
and strong,
in the clothes
of a modern
man, he proclaims
himself.

Say to all foemen:
You can't keep me down!
Tear off the garments
That make me a clown!

Rise from the bottom,
Out of the slime!
Look at the stars yonder
Calling through time!

Cry to the world
That all might understand:
I was once a black clown
But now—
I'm a man!

The Big-Timer

A moral poem to be rendered by a man in a straw hat with a bright band, a diamond ring, cigarette holder, and a cane, to the music of piano or orchestra.

THE MOOD
Syncopated
music.
Telling his
story
in a hard,
brazen,
cynical
fashion.
Careless,
and half-
defiant
echoes
of the
"St. James
Infirmary"
as the music
takes
on a

THE POEM
Who am I?
It ain't so deep:
I'm the guy the home folks call—
The Black Sheep.

I ran away.
Went to the city.
Look at me now and
Laugh—or take pity.

I'm the bad egg, see!
Didn't turn out right.
My people disowned me—
So I'm hustlin' in the night.

Drinkin' and gamblin' now,
And livin' on gals.
Red-hot—that's me,
With a lot o' sporty pals.

*blues
strain,
gradually
returning to
a sort of
barrel-house
jazz.
Showing-off.
Strutting
about
proudly,
bragging
and
boasting
like a
cheap
bully. But
suddenly
looking ahead:
shrugging his
shoulders
at fate.
Accepting
his position—
but inside
himself un-
happy and blue.
Hiding his
discontent
as thoughts
of a
better life
overcome him.
Assuming
a false
and bragging
self-assurance,*

Spendin' money like water.
Drinkin' life like wine.
Not livin' like I oughter,
But—ain't my life mine?

I got a high-yaller.
Got a diamond ring.
I got a furnished-up flat,
And all that kind o' thing.

I got a big car
And I steps on the gas,
And whoever don't like it
Just gimme some sass,

'Cause I carries a switch-blade
And I swing it a-hummin',
And if I don't get you goin',
I'll cut you down comin'.

You say I'll meet a bad endin', heh?
Well, maybe I will.
But while I'm livin'—I'm livin'!
And when I'm dead—I'll keep still.

I'm a first class hustler,
Rounder and sport.
Sometimes I'm settin' pretty,
And again money's short.

But if I wanted to go straight
I'd starve and—oh, well—
I'm just a good-timer
On my road to hell.

Lots of old schoolmates are married now;
Home, kids, and everything fine.
But I ain't got nothin' real
That I can call mine.

But don't let it matter to you,
'Cause I'm all right.
I'm eatin' and lovin',
And holdin' things tight.

and a
pretended
strength he
doesn't
really feel.
Gay,
loud,
unhappy
jazz.
Baring
his inner
heartaches
and loneliness
to the
ironic
gaiety of
the music.
Then
pulling
himself together,
boasting
loudly again,
but realizing
within
the tragic
emptiness
of his
life.

So don't worry 'bout me,
Folks, down yonder at home.
I guess I can stand the racket
And fight it out alone.

I guess I know what I'm up against.
I don't cry over troubles.
Look 'em in the face and
Bust 'em like bubbles.

I turn on the radio,
Mix up a drink,
Make lots o' noise,
Then I don't have to think.

Call in a gang o' women
And let 'em have my money,
And forget that they lyin'
When they callin' me honey.

So what's the use o' worryin'
Or thinkin' at all?
We only got one life
And I guess that one's all—

So I'm takin' it easy
And I don't give a damn—
I'm just a big-timer,
That's all I am!

That's . . . all . . . I . . . am.

The Negro Mother

Children, I come back today
To tell you a story of the long dark way
That I had to climb, that I had to know
In order that the race might live and grow.

Look at my face—dark as the night—
Yet shining like the sun with love's true light.
I am the child they stole from the sand
Three hundred years ago in Africa's land.
I am the dark girl who crossed the wide sea
Carrying in my body the seed of the free.
I am the woman who worked in the field
Bringing the cotton and the corn to yield.
I am the one who labored as a slave,
Beaten and mistreated for the work that I gave—
Children sold away from me, husband sold, too.
No safety, no love, no respect was I due.
Three hundred years in the deepest South:
But God put a song and a prayer in my mouth.
God put a dream like steel in my soul.
Now, through my children, I'm reaching the goal.
Now, through my children, young and free,
I realize the blessings denied to me.
I couldn't read then. I couldn't write.
I had nothing, back there in the night.
Sometimes, the valley was filled with tears,
But I kept trudging on through the lonely years.
Sometimes, the road was hot with sun,
But I had to keep on till my work was done:
I *had* to keep on! No stopping for me—
I was the seed of the coming Free.
I nourished the dream that nothing could smother
Deep in my breast—the Negro mother.
I had only hope then, but now through you,
Dark ones of today, my dreams must come true:
All you dark children in the world out there,
Remember my sweat, my pain, my despair.
Remember my years, heavy with sorrow—
And make of those years a torch for tomorrow.
Make of my past a road to the light

Out of the darkness, the ignorance, the night.
Lift high my banner out of the dust.
Stand like free men supporting my trust.
Believe in the right, let none push you back.
Remember the whip and the slaver's track.
Remember how the strong in struggle and strife
Still bar you the way, and deny you life—
But march ever forward, breaking down bars.
Look ever upward at the sun and the stars.
Oh, my dark children, may my dreams and my prayers
Impel you forever up the great stairs—
For I will be with you till no white brother
Dares keep down the children of the Negro mother.

Dark Youth of the U.S.A.

A recitation to be delivered by a Negro boy, bright, clean, and neatly
dressed, carrying his books to school.

Sturdy I stand, books in my hand—
Today's dark child, tomorrow's strong man:
    The hope of my race
    To mould a place
In America's magic land.

American am I, none can deny:
He who oppresses me, him I defy!
    I am Dark Youth
    Seeking the truth
Of a free life beneath our great sky.
Long a part of the Union's heart—
Years ago at the nation's start
    Attucks died
    That right might abide
And strength to our land impart.

To be wise and strong, then, studying long,
Seeking the knowledge that rights all wrong—
    That is my mission.
Lifting my race to its rightful place
Till beauty and pride fills each dark face
    Is my ambition.

So I climb toward tomorrow, out of past sorrow,
    Treading the modern way
With the White and the Black whom nothing holds back—
    The American Youth of today.

Pennsylvania Station

The Pennsylvania Station in New York
Is like some vast basilica of old
That towers above the terror of the dark
As bulwark and protection to the soul.
Now people who are hurrying alone
And those who come in crowds from far away
Pass through this great concourse of steel and stone
To trains, or else from trains out into day.
And as in great basilicas of old
The search was ever for a dream of God,
So here the search is still within each soul
Some seed to find to root in earthly sod,
Some seed to find that sprouts a holy tree
To glorify the earth—and you—and me.

Ph.D.

He never was a silly little boy
Who whispered in the class or threw spit balls,
Or pulled the hair of silly little girls,
Or disobeyed in any way the laws
That made the school a place of decent order
Where books were read and sums were proven true
And paper maps that showed the land and water
Were held up as the real wide world to you.
Always, he kept his eyes upon his books:
And now he has grown to be a man
He is surprised that everywhere he looks
Life rolls in waves he cannot understand,
And all the human world is vast and strange—
And quite beyond his Ph.D.'s small range.

Good Morning Revolution

Good-morning, Revolution:
    You're the very best friend
    I ever had.
We gonna pal around together from now on.
Say, listen, Revolution:
You know, the boss where I used to work,
The guy that gimme the air to cut down expenses,
He wrote a long letter to the papers about you:
Said you was a trouble maker, a alien-enemy,
In other words a son-of-a-bitch.
He called up the police
And told 'em to watch out for a guy
Named Revolution.

You see,
The boss knows you're my friend.
He sees us hangin' out together.
He knows we're hungry, and ragged,
And ain't got a damn thing in this world—
And are gonna do something about it.

The boss's got all he needs, certainly,
    Eats swell,
    Owns a lotta houses,
    Goes vacationin',
    Breaks strikes,
    Runs politics, bribes police,
    Pays off congress,
    And struts all over the earth—

But me, I ain't never had enough to eat.
Me, I ain't never been warm in winter.
Me, I ain't never known security—
All my life, been livin' hand to mouth,
    Hand to mouth.

Listen, Revolution,
    We're buddies, see—
    Together,
    We can take everything:
    Factories, arsenals, houses, ships,
    Railroads, forests, fields, orchards,
    Bus lines, telegraphs, radios,
    (Jesus! Raise hell with radios!)
    Steel mills, coal mines, oil wells, gas,
    All the tools of production,
    (Great day in the morning!)
    Everything—
And turn 'em over to the people who work.
Rule and run 'em for us people who work.

Boy! Them radios—
Broadcasting that very first morning to USSR:
Another member the International Soviet's done come
Greetings to the Socialist Soviet Republics
Hey you rising workers everywhere greetings—
    And we'll sign it: *Germany*
    Sign it: *China*
    Sign it: *Africa*
    Sign it: *Poland*
    Sign it: *Italy*
    Sign it: *America*
    Sign it with my one name: *Worker*
On that day when no one will be hungry, cold, oppressed,
Anywhere in the world again.

    That's our job!

    I been starvin' too long,
    Ain't you?

    Let's go, Revolution!

Always the Same

It is the same everywhere for me:
On the docks at Sierra Leone,
In the cotton fields of Alabama,
In the diamond mines of Kimberley,
On the coffee hills of Haiti,
The banana lands of Central America,
The streets of Harlem,
And the cities of Morocco and Tripoli.

Black:
Exploited, beaten and robbed,

Shot and killed.
Blood running into

> Dollars
> Pounds
> Francs
> Pesetas
> Lire

For the wealth of the exploiters—
Blood that never comes back to me again.
Better that my blood
Runs into the deep channels of Revolution,
Runs into the strong hands of Revolution,
Stains all flags red,
Drives me away from

> Sierra Leone
> Kimberley
> Alabama
> Haiti
> Central America
> Harlem
> Morocco
> Tripoli

And all the black lands everywhere.
The force that kills,
The power that robs,
And the greed that does not care.

Better that my blood makes one with the blood
Of all the struggling workers in the world—
Till every land is free of
> Dollar robbers
> Pound robbers

Franc robbers
Peseta robbers
Lire robbers
Life robbers—

Until the Red Armies of the International Proletariat
Their faces, black, white, olive, yellow, brown,
Unite to raise the blood-red flag that
Never will come down!

Goodbye Christ

Listen, Christ,
You did alright in your day, I reckon—
But that day's gone now.
They ghosted you up a swell story, too,
Called it Bible—
But it's dead now,
The popes and the preachers've
Made too much money from it.
They've sold you to too many

Kings, generals, robbers, and killers—
Even to the Tzar and the Cossacks,
Even to Rockefeller's Church,
Even to THE SATURDAY EVENING POST.
You ain't no good no more.
They've pawned you
Till you've done wore out.

Goodbye,
Christ Jesus Lord God Jehova,
Beat it on away from here now.
Make way for a new guy with no religion at all—
A real guy named

Marx Communist Lenin Peasant Stalin Worker ME—

I said, ME!

Go ahead on now,
You're getting in the way of things, Lord.
And please take Saint Gandhi with you when you go,
And Saint Pope Pius,
And Saint Aimee McPherson,
And big black Saint Becton
Of the Consecrated Dime.
And step on the gas, Christ!
Move!

Don't be so slow about movin'!
The world is mine from now on—
And nobody's gonna sell ME
To a king, or a general,
Or a millionaire.

Irish Wake

In the dark they fell a-crying
For the dead who'd gone away,
And you could hear the drowsy wailing
Of those compelled to stay—
But when the sun rose making
All the dooryard bright and clear
The mourners got up smiling,
Happy they were here.

Reasons Why

Just because I loves you—
That's de reason why
Ma soul is full of color
Like de wings of a butterfly.

Just because I loves you
That's de reason why
Ma heart's a fluttering aspen leaf
When you pass by.

The Town of Scottsboro

Scottsboro's just a little place:
No shame is writ across its face—
Its court, too weak to stand against a mob,
Its people's heart, too small to hold a sob.

Columbia

Columbia,
My dear girl,
You really haven't been a virgin for so long
It's ludicrous to keep up the pretext.
You're terribly involved in world assignations
And everybody knows it.
You've slept with all the big powers
In military uniforms,
And you've taken the sweet life
Of all the little brown fellows
In loin cloths and cotton trousers.
When they've resisted,

You've yelled, "Rape,"
At the top of your voice
And called for the middies
To beat them up for not being gentlemen
And liking your crooked painted mouth.
(You must think the moons of Hawaii
Disguise your ugliness.)
Really,
You're getting a little too old,
Columbia,
To be so naive, and so coy.
Being one of the world's big vampires,
Why don't you come on out and say so
Like Japan, and England, and France,
And all the other nymphomaniacs of power
Who've long since dropped their
Smoke-screens of innocence
To sit frankly on a bed of bombs?

O, sweet mouth of India,
And Africa,
Manchuria, and Haiti.

Columbia,
You darling,
Don't shoot!
I'll kiss you!

Letter to the Academy

The gentlemen who have got to be classics and are now old with
    beards (or dead and in their graves) will kindly come forward and
    speak upon the subject

Of the Revolution. I mean the gentlemen who wrote lovely books
about the defeat of the flesh and the triumph of the spirit that sold in
the hundreds of thousands and are studied in the high schools and
read by the best people will kindly come forward and

Speak about the Revolution—where the flesh triumphs (as well as the
spirit) and the hungry belly eats, and there are no best people, and
the poor are mighty and no longer poor, and the young by the
hundreds of thousands are free from hunger to grow and study and
love and propagate, bodies and souls unchained without My Lord
saying a commoner shall never marry my daughter or the Rabbi
crying cursed be the mating of Jews and Gentiles or Kipling writing
never the twain shall meet—

For the twain have met. But please—all you gentlemen with beards
who are so wise and old and who write better than we do and whose
souls have triumphed (in spite of hungers and wars and the evils
about you) and whose books have soared in calmness and beauty
aloof from the struggle to the library shelves and the desks of
students and who are now classics—come forward and speak upon

The subject of the Revolution.

We want to know what in the hell you'd say?

Song of the Revolution

Sing me a song of the Revolution
Marching like fire over the world,
Weaving from the earth its bright red banner
For the hands of the masses to unfurl.

Sing me a song of the Revolution
Drowning the past with a thunderous shout:

Filled with the strength of youth and laughter,
And never the echo of a doubt.

O mighty roll of the Revolution,
Ending the centuries of bloody strife,
Ending the tricks of kings and liars,
Big with the laughter of a new life.

Breaking the bonds of the darker races,
Breaking the chains that have held for years,
Breaking the barriers dividing the people,
Smashing the gods of terror and tears,

Cutting, O flame of the Revolution,
Fear from the world like a surgeon's knife,
So that the children of all creation
Waken, at last, to the joy of life.

Black Workers

The bees work.
Their work is taken from them.
We are like the bees—
But it won't last
Forever.

Black Dancers

We
Who have nothing to lose
Must sing and dance
Before the riches
Of the world

Overcome
Us.

We
Who have nothing to lose
Must laugh and dance
Lest our laughter
Goes from
Us.

Wait

PICKERS	I am the Silent One,	MEERUT
CHAPEI	Saying nothing,	HAITI
	Knowing no words to write,	
FORD	Feeling only the bullets	KOREA
STRIKERS	And the hunger	CHILD
	And the stench of gas	
ALABAMA	Dying.	LABOR
NEGROES	And nobody knows my name	SUGAR
	But someday,	
CUBA	I shall raise my hand	HAITI
	And break the heads of you	
UNEMPLOYED	Who starve me.	BONUS
MILLIONS	I shall raise my hand	KOREA
	And smash the spines of you	
MEERUT	Who shoot me.	MEERUT
CHILD		CHILD
	I shall take your guns	
LABOR	And turn them on you.	LABOR
SCOTTSBORO		BONUS
	Starting with the bankers and	
GERMAN	the bosses	HAITI
	Traders and missionaries	
COMMUNISTS	Who pay the militarists	KOREA
POOR	Who pay the soldiers	SUGAR
	Who back the police	
FARMERS	Who kill me—	CHILD
	And break my strikes	
BLACK	And break my rising—	LABOR

AFRICA

GRAPE

PICKERS

JAPANESE

CONSCRIPTS

JOHANNESBURG

MINERS

HAITI

BONUS

KOREA

BLACK

HAITI

SUGAR

MEERUT

I, silently,
And without a single learned word
Shall begin the slaughter
That will end my hunger
And your bullets
And the gas of capitalism
And make the world
My own.
When that is done,
I shall find words to speak

Wait!

HAITI UNEMPLOYED MILLIONS CALIFORNIA CHERRY PICKERS STRIKING
MINERS ALABAMA SUGAR BEET WORKERS INDIAN MASSES SCOTTSBORO
SHANGHAI COOLIES PATTERSON SUGAR BEET WORKERS COLONIAL
ASIA FRICK'S MINERS CUBA POOR FARMERS JAPANESE CONSCRIPTS
WORKERS JOHANNESBURG MINERS CHAPEI ALABAMA NEGROES
OXNARD SUGAR BEET WORKERS INDIAN MASSES BONUS MARCHERS
FORD STRIKERS HAITI

Revolution

Great mob that knows no fear—
Come here!
And raise your hand
Against this man
Of iron and steel and gold
Who's bought and sold
You—
Each one—
For the last thousand years,
Come here,
Great mob that has no fear,
And tear him limb from limb,
Split his golden throat
Ear to ear,

And end his time forever,
Now—
This year—
Great mob that knows no fear.

Cubes

In the days of the broken cubes of Picasso
And in the days of the broken songs of the young men
A little too drunk to sing
And the young women
A little too unsure of love to love—
I met on the boulevards of Paris
An African from Senegal.

God
Knows why the French
Amuse themselves bringing to Paris
Negroes from Senegal.

It's the old game of the boss and the bossed,
   boss and the bossed,
      amused
        and
      amusing,
   worked and working,
Behind the cubes of black and white,
         black and white,
   black and white
But since it is the old game,
For fun
They give him the three old prostitutes of
    France—
Liberty, Equality, Fraternity—

And all three of 'em sick
In spite of the tax to the government
And the legal houses
And the doctors
And the *Marseillaise.*

Of course, the young African from Senegal
Carries back from Paris
A little more disease
To spread among the black girls in the palm huts.
He brings them as a gift
      disease—
From light to darkness
         disease—
From the boss to the bossed
           disease—
From the game of black and white
     disease—
From the city of the broken cubes of Picasso
     d
       i
     s
   e
     a
       s
     e

One More "S" in the U.S.A.

Put one more s in the U.S.A.
To make it Soviet.
One more s in the U.S.A.
Oh, we'll live to see it yet.
When the land belongs to the farmers

And the factories to the working men—
The U.S.A. when we take control
Will be the U.S.S.A. then.

Now across the water in Russia
They have a big U.S.S.R.
The fatherland of the Soviets—
But that is mighty far
From New York, or Texas, or California, too.
So listen, fellow workers,
This is what we have to do.

   Put one more S in the U.S.A.
    [Repeat chorus]

But we can't win by just talking.
So let us take things in our hand.
Then down and away with the bosses' sway—
Hail Communistic land.
So stand up in battle and wave our flag on high,
And shout out fellow workers
Our new slogan in the sky:

   Put one more S in the U.S.A.

But we can't join hands together
So long as whites are lynching black,
So black and white in one union fight
And get on the right track.
By Texas, or Georgia, or Alabama led
Come together, fellow workers
Black and white can all be red:

   Put one more S in the U.S.A.

Oh, the bankers they all are planning
For another great big war.

To make them rich from the worker's dead,
That's all the war is for.
So if you don't want to see bullets holding sway
Then come on, all you workers,
And join our fight today:

> Put one more S in the U.S.A.
> To make it Soviet.
> One more S in the U.S.A.
> Oh, we'll live to see it yet.
> When the land belongs to the farmers
> And the factories to the working men—
> The U.S.A. when we take control
> Will be the U.S.S.A. then.

Ballad of Roosevelt

The pot was empty,
The cupboard was bare.
I said, Papa,
What's the matter here?
I'm waitin' on Roosevelt, son,
Roosevelt, Roosevelt,
Waitin' on Roosevelt, son.

The rent was due
And the lights was out.
I said, Tell me, Mama,
What's it all about?
We're waitin' on Roosevelt, son,
Roosevelt, Roosevelt,
Just waitin' on Roosevelt.

Sister got sick
And the doctor wouldn't come

Cause we couldn't pay him
The proper sum—
A-waitin' on Roosevelt,
Roosevelt, Roosevelt,
A-waitin' on Roosevelt.

Then one day
They put us out o' the house.
Ma and Pa was
Meek as a mouse
Still waitin' on Roosevelt,
Roosevelt, Roosevelt.

But when they felt those
Cold winds blow
And didn't have no
Place to go
Pa said, I'm tired
O' waitin' on Roosevelt,
Roosevelt, Roosevelt.
Damn tired o' waitin' on Roosevelt.

I can't git a job
And I can't git no grub.
Backbone and navel's
Doin' the belly-rub—
A-waitin' on Roosevelt,
Roosevelt, Roosevelt.

And a lot o' other folks
What's hungry and cold
Done stopped believin'
What they been told
By Roosevelt,
Roosevelt, Roosevelt—

Cause the pot's still empty,
And the cupboard's still bare,
And you can't build a bungalow
Out o' air—
Mr. Roosevelt, listen!
What's the matter here?

Call of Ethiopia

Ethiopia
Lift your night-dark face,
   Abyssinian
   Son of Sheba's race!
   Your palm trees tall
   And your mountains high
   Are shade and shelter
   To men who die
   For freedom's sake—
   But in the wake of your sacrifice
   May all Africa arise
   With blazing eyes and night-dark face
   In answer to the call of Sheba's race:

   Ethiopias free!
   Be like me,
   All of Africa,
   Arise and be free!
   All you black peoples,
   Be free! Be free!

Air Raid over Harlem

Scenario for a Little Black Movie

Who you gonna put in it?
Me.
Who the hell are you?
Harlem.
Alright, then.

AIR RAID OVER HARLEM

You're not talkin' 'bout Harlem, are you?
That's where my home is,
My bed is, my woman is, my kids is!
Harlem, that's where I live!
Look at my streets
Full of black and brown and
Yellow and high-yellow
Jokers like me.
Lenox, Seventh, Edgecombe, 145th.
Listen,
Hear 'em talkin' and laughin'?
Bombs over Harlem'd kill
People like me—
Kill ME!
Sure, I know
The Ethiopian war broke out last night:
BOMBS OVER HARLEM
Cops on every corner
Most of 'em white
COPS IN HARLEM
Guns and billy-clubs
Double duty in Harlem
Walking in pairs
Under every light

Their faces
WHITE
In Harlem
And mixed in with 'em
A black cop or two
For the sake of the vote in Harlem
GUGSA A TRAITOR TOO
No, sir,
I ain't talkin' 'bout you,
Mister Policeman!
No, indeed!
I know we got to keep
ORDER OVER HARLEM
Where the black millions sleep
Shepherds over Harlem
Their armed watch keep
Lest Harlem stirs in its sleep
And maybe remembers
And remembering forgets
To be peaceful and quiet
And has sudden fits
Of raising a black fist
Out of the dark
And that black fist
Becomes a red spark
PLANES OVER HARLEM
Bombs over Harlem
You're just making up
A fake funny picture, ain't you?
Not real, not real?
Did you ever taste blood
From an iron heel
Planted in your mouth
In the slavery-time South
Where to whip a nigger's

Easy as hell—
And not even a *living* nigger
Has a tale to tell
Lest the kick of a boot
Baring more blood to his mouth
In the slavery-time South
And a long billy-club
Split his head wide
And a white hand draw
A gun from its side
And send bullets splaying
Through the streets of Harlem
Where the dead're laying
Lest you stir in your sleep
And remember something
You'd best better keep
In the dark, in the dark
Where the ugly things hide
Under the white lights
With guns by their side
In Harlem?

Say, what are yuh tryin' to do?
Start a riot?
You keep quiet!
You niggers keep quiet!

BLACK WORLD
Never wake up
Lest you knock over the cup
Of gold that the men who
Keep order guard so well
And then—well, then
There'd be hell

To pay
And bombs over Harlem

AIR RAID OVER HARLEM

Bullets through Harlem
And someday
A sleeping giant waking
To snatch bombs from the sky
And push the sun up with a loud cry
Of to hell with the cops on the corners at night
Armed to the teeth under the light
Lest Harlem see red
And suddenly sit on the edge of its bed
And shake the whole world with a new dream
As the squad cars come and the sirens scream
And a big black giant snatches bombs from the sky
And picks up a cop and lets him fly
Into the dust of the Jimcrow past
And laughs and Hollers
Kiss my
!x!&!

Hey!
Scenario for a Little Black Movie,
You say?
A RED MOVIE TO MR. HEARST
Black and white workers united as one
In a city where
There'll never be
Air raids over Harlem
FOR THE WORKERS ARE FREE

What workers are free?
THE BLACK AND WHITE WORKERS—
You and me!

Looky here, everybody!
Look at me!

I'M HARLEM!

Broadcast on Ethiopia

The little fox is still.
  The dogs of war have made their kill.

  Addis Ababa
  Across the headlines all year long.
  Ethiopia—
  Tragi-song for the news reels.
  Haile
  With his slaves, his dusky wiles,
  His second-hand planes like a child's,
  But he has no gas—so he cannot last.
  Poor little joker with no poison gas!
  Thus his people now may learn
  How Il Duce makes butter from an empty churn
  To butter the bread
  (If bread there be)
  Of civilization's misery.

    MISTER CHRISTOPHER COLUMBUS

DJIBOUTI, French Somaliland, May 4 (AP)—Emperor Haile Selassie
and imperial family, in flight from his crumbling empire, reached the
sanctuary of French soil and a British destroyer today. . . .

    HE USED RHYTHM FOR HIS COMPASS

  Hunter, hunter, running, too—
  Look what's after you:

PARIS, May 4 (UP)—COMMUNISTS TOP FRANCE'S SWEEP
LEFT. Minister of Colonies Defeated. Rise From 10 to 85 Seats.

France ain't Italy!

No, but Italy's cheated
When *any* Minister anywhere's
Defeated by Communists.
Goddamn! I swear!
Hitler,
Tear your hair!
Mussolini,
Grit your teeth!
Civilization's gone to hell!
Major Bowes, ring your bell!

   (Gong!)

Station XYZW broadcasting:
MISTER CHRISTOPHER COLOMBO
Just made a splendid kill.
The British Legation stands solid on its hill
The natives run wild in the streets.
The fox is still.

Addis Ababa
In headlines all year long.
Ethiopia—tragi-song.

White Man

Sure I know you!
You're a White Man.
I'm a Negro.
You take all the best jobs

And leave us the garbage cans to empty
and
The halls to clean.
You have a good time in a big house at
Palm Beach
And rent us the back alleys
And the dirty slums.
You enjoy Rome—
And *take* Ethiopia.
White Man! White Man!
Let Louis Armstrong play it—
And you copyright it
And make the money.
You're the smart guy, White Man!
You got everything!
But now,
I hear your name ain't really White
Man.
I hear it's something
Marx wrote down
Fifty years ago—
That rich people don't like to read.
Is that true, White Man?
Is your name in a book
Called the *Communist Manifesto?*
Is your name spelled
C-A-P-I-T-A-L-I-S-T?
Are you always a White Man?
Huh?

Roar China!

Roar, China!
Roar, old lion of the East!
Snort fire, yellow dragon of the Orient,
Tired at last of being bothered.
Since when did you ever steal anything
From anybody,
Sleepy wise old beast
Known as the porcelain-maker,
Known as the poem-maker,
Known as maker of firecrackers?
A long time since you cared
About taking other people's lands
Away from them.
THEY must've thought you didn't care
About your own land either—
So THEY came with gunboats,
Set up Concessions,
Zones of influence,
International Settlements,
Missionary houses,
Banks,
And Jim Crow Y.M.C.A.'s.
THEY beat you with malacca canes
And dared you to raise your head—
Except to cut it off.
Even the yellow men came
To take what the white men
Hadn't already taken.
The yellow men dropped bombs on Chapei.
The yellow men called you the same names
The white men did:
  Dog! Dog! Dog!
  Coolie dog!

Red! . . . Lousy red!
Red coolie dog!
And in the end you had no place
To make your porcelain,
Write your poems,
Or shoot your firecrackers on holidays.
In the end you had no peace
Or calm left at all.
PRESIDENT, KING, MIKADO
Thought you really were a dog.
THEY kicked you daily
Via radiophone, via cablegram,
Via gunboats in her harbor,
Via malacca canes.
THEY thought you were a tame lion.
A sleepy, easy, tame old lion!
   Ha! Ha!
   Haaa-aa-a! . . . Ha!
Laugh, little coolie boy on the docks of Shanghai, laugh!
   You're no tame lion.
Laugh, red generals in the hills of Sian-kiang, laugh!
   You're no tame lion.
Laugh, child slaves in the factories of the foreigners!
   You're no tame lion.
Laugh—and roar, China! Time to spit fire!
Open your mouth, old dragon of the East.
To swallow up the gunboats in the Yangtse!
Swallow up the foreign planes in your sky!
Eat bullets, old maker of firecrackers—
And spit out freedom in the face of your enemies!
Break the chains of the East,
   Little coolie boy!
Break the chains of the East,
   Red generals!
Break the chains of the East,

Child slaves in the factories!
Smash the iron gates of the Concessions!
Smash the pious doors of the missionary houses!
Smash the revolving doors of the Jim Crow Y.M.C.A.'s.
Crush the enemies of land and bread and freedom!
    Stand up and roar, China!
    You know what you want!
    The only way to get it is
    To take it!
    Roar, China!

Note in Music

Life is for the living.
Death is for the dead.
Let life be like music.
And death a note unsaid.

Search

All life is but the climbing of a hill
To seek the sun that ranges far beyond
Confused with stars and lesser lights anon,
And planets where the darkness reigneth still.

All life is but the seeking for that sun
That never lets one living atom die—
That flames beyond the circles of the eye
Where Never and Forever are as one.

And seeking always through this human span
That spreads its drift of years beneath the sky
Confused with living, goeth simple man

Unknowing and unknown into the Why—
The Why that flings itself beyond the Sun
And back in space to where Time was begun.

Letter from Spain

Addressed to Alabama

>   Lincoln Battalion,
>   International Brigades,
>   November Something, 1937.

Dear Brother at home:

We captured a wounded Moor today.
He was just as dark as me.
I said, Boy, what you been doin' here
Fightin' against the free?

He answered something in a language
I couldn't understand.
But somebody told me he was sayin'
They nabbed him in his land

And made him join the fascist army
And come across to Spain.
And he said he had a feelin'
He'd never get back home again.

He said he had a feelin'
This whole thing wasn't right.
He said he didn't know
The folks he had to fight.

And as he lay there dying
In a village we had taken,

I looked across to Africa
And seed foundations shakin'.

Cause if a free Spain wins this war,
The colonies, too, are free—
Then something wonderful'll happen
To them Moors as dark as me.

I said, I guess that's why old England
And I reckon Italy, too,
Is afraid to let a workers' Spain
Be too good to me and you—

Cause they got slaves in Africa—
And they don't want 'em to be free.
Listen, Moorish prisoner, hell!
Here, shake hands with me!

I knelt down there beside him,
And I took his hand—
But the wounded Moor was dyin'
And he didn't understand.

> Salud,
> Johnny

Postcard from Spain

Addressed to Alabama

> Lincoln-Washington Battalion,
> April, 1938

Dear Folks at home:

I went out this mornin'
Old shells was a-fallin'

Whistlin' and a-fallin'
When I went out this mornin'.

I'm way over here
A long ways from home,
Over here in Spanish country
But I don't feel alone.

Folks over here don't treat me
Like white folks used to do.
When I was home they treated me
Just like they treatin' you.

I don't think things'll ever
Be like that again:
I done met up with folks
Who'll fight for me now
Like I'm fightin' now for Spain.

Salud,
Johnny

August 19th . . .

A Poem for Clarence Morris

What flag will fly for me
When I die?
What flag of red and white and
    blue,
Half-mast, against the sky?
I'm not the President,
Nor the Honorable So-and-So.
But only one of the
Scottsboro Boys
Doomed "by law" to go.

August 19th is the date.
Put it in your book.
The date that I must keep with
    death.
Would you like to come and look?
You will see a black boy die.
Would you like to come and cry?
Maybe tears politely shed
Help the dead.
Or better still, they may help you—
For if you let the "law" kill me,
Are you free?
August 19th is the date.
Clarence Norris is my name.
The sentence, against me,
Against you, the same.
August 19th is the date.
Thunder in the sky.
In Alabama
A young black boy will die.
August 19th is the date.
Judges in high places
Still preserve their dignity
And dispose of cases.
August 19th is the date.
Rich people sit and fan
And sip cool drinks and do no work—
Yet they rule the land.
August 19th is the date.
The electric chair.
Swimmers on cool beaches
With their bodies bare.
August 19th is the date.
European tours.
Summer camps for the kids.

If they are yours.
Me, I never had no kids.
I never had no wife.
August 19th is the date.
To take my life.
August 19th is the date.
Will your church bells ring?
August 19th is the date.
Will the choir sing?
August 19th is the date.
Will the ball games stop?
August 19th is the date.
Will the jazz bands play?
August 19th is the date.
When I go away.
August 19th is the date.
Thunder in the sky.
August 19th is the date.
Scottsboro Boy must die.
August 19th is the date.
Judges in high places—
August 19th is the date—
Still dispose of cases.
August 19th is the date.
Rich people sit and fan.
August 19th is the date.
Who shall rule our land?
August 19th is the date.
Swimmers on cool beaches.
August 19th is the date.
                    World!
stop *all the leeches*
That suck your life away and mine.
                    World!
stop *all the leeches*

That use their power to strangle
   hope,
That make of the law a lyncher's
   rope,
That drop their bombs on China
   and Spain,
That have no pity for hunger or
   pain,
That always, forever, close the door
Against the likes of me, the poor,
AUGUST 19th IS THE DATE.
What flag will fly for me?
AUGUST 19th IS THE DATE.
So deep my grave will be.
AUGUST 19th IS THE DATE.
I'm not the honorable So-and-So.
AUGUST 19th IS THE DATE.
Just a poor boy doomed to go.
AUGUST 19th IS THE DATE.

AUGUST 19th IS THE DATE.
Can you make death wait?
AUGUST 19th IS THE DATE.
Will you let me die?
AUGUST 19th IS THE DATE.
Can we make death wait?
AUGUST 19th IS THE DATE.
Will you let me die?
AUGUST 19th IS THE DATE.
AUGUST 19th IS THE DATE.
AUGUST 19th . . . AUGUST 19th . . .
AUGUST 19th . . . AUGUST 19th . . .
   AUGUST 19th . . .

Moscow

Here are the red flags
That wave
In the bright silver glory
Of the dawn—
The red flags
That ask no pardon
Of the past—
Dead and gone.

Madrid

Damaged by shells, many of the clocks on the public buildings in Madrid
have stopped. At night, the streets are pitch dark.

—*News Item*

Put out the lights and stop the clocks.
Let time stand still.
Again man mocks himself
And all his human will to build and grow.
Madrid!
The fact and symbol of man's woe.
Madrid!
Time's end and throw-back,
Birth of darkness,
Years of light reduced:
The ever minus of the brute,
The nothingness of barren land
And stone and metal,
Emptyness of gold,
The dullness of a bill of sale:
BOUGHT AND PAID FOR! SOLD!
Stupidity of hours that do not move

Because all clocks are stopped.
Blackness of nights that do not see
Because all lights are out.
Madrid
Beneath the bullets!
Madrid
Beneath the bombing planes!
Madrid
In the fearful dark!

Oh, mind of man!
So long to make a light
of fire,
 of oil,
  of gas,
And now electric rays.
So long to make a clock
Of sun-dial,
 sand-dial,
  figures,
And now two hands that mark the hours.
Oh, mind of man!
So long to struggle upward out of darkness
To a measurement of time—
And now:
These guns,
These brainless killers in the hills
Trained on Madrid
To stop the clocks in the towers
And shatter all their faces
Into a million bits of nothingness
In the city
That will not bow its head
To darkness and to greed again:
That dares to dream a cleaner dream!

Oh, mind of man
Moulded into a metal shell—
Left-overs of the past
That rain dull hell and misery
On the world again—
Have your way
And stop the clocks!
Bomb out the lights!
And mock yourself!
Mock all the rights of those
Who live like decent folk.
Let guns alone salute
The wisdom of our age
With dusty powder marks
On yet another page of history.
Let there be no sense of time,
Nor measurement of light and dark.
In fact, no light at all!
Let mankind fall
Into the deepest pit that ignorance can dig
For us all!
Descent is quick.
To rise again is slow.
In the darkness of her broken clocks,
Madrid cries NO!
In the timeless midnight of the Fascist guns,
Madrid cries No!
To all the killers of man's dreams,
Madrid cries NO!

> To break that NO apart
> Will be to break the human heart.

Beauty

They give to beauty here—
The same as everywhere—
Adulation, but no care.

Song for Ourselves

Czechoslovakia lynched on a swastika cross!
   Blow, bitter winds, blow!
   Blow, bitter winds, blow!
Nails in her hands and nails in her feet,
   Left to die slow!
   Left to die slow!
Czechoslovakia! Ethiopia! Spain!
   One after another!
   One after another!
Where will the long snake of greed strike again?
   Will it be here, brother?

Air Raid: Barcelona

Black smoke of sound
Curls against the midnight sky.

Deeper than a whistle,
Louder than a cry,
Worse than a scream
Tangled in the wail
Of a nightmare dream,
   The siren
Of the air raid sounds.

Flames and bombs and
Death in the ear!
The siren announces
Planes drawing near.
Down from bedrooms
Stumble women in gowns.
Men, half-dressed,
Carrying children rush down.
Up in the sky-lanes
Against the stars
A flock of death birds
Whose wings are steel bars
Fill the sky with a low dull roar
Of a plane,
        two planes,
                three planes,
                        five planes,
                                or more.
The anti-aircraft guns bark into space.
The searchlights make wounds
On the night's dark face.
The siren's wild cry
Like a hollow scream
Echoes out of hell in a nightmare dream.
    Then the BOMBS fall!
All other noises are nothing at all
    When the first BOMBS fall.
All other noises are suddenly still
    When the BOMBS fall.
All other noises are deathly still
As blood spatters the wall
And the whirling sound
Of the iron star of death
Comes hurtling down.
No other noises can be heard

As a child's life goes up
In the night like a bird.
Swift pursuit planes
Dart over the town,
Steel bullets fly
Slitting the starry silk
   Of the sky:
A bomber's brought down
In flames orange and blue,
And the night's all red
Like blood, too.
   The last BOMB falls.

The death birds wheel East
To their lairs again
Leaving iron eggs
In the streets of Spain.
With wings like black cubes
Against the far dawn,
The stench of their passage
Remains when they're gone.
In what was a courtyard
A child weeps alone.

Men uncover bodies
From ruins of stone.

Poet to Patron

What right has anyone to say
That I
Must throw out pieces of my heart
For pay?

For bread that helps to make
My heart beat true,
I must sell myself
To you?

A factory shift's better,
A week's meagre pay,
Than a perfumed note asking:
What poems today?

Red Clay Blues

(by Langston Hughes and Richard Wright)

I miss that red clay, Lawd, I
Need to feel it in my shoes.
Says miss that red clay, Lawd, I
Need to feel it in my shoes.
I want to get to Georgia cause I
Got them red clay blues.

Pavement's hard on my feet, I'm
Tired o' this concrete street.
Pavement's hard on my feet, I'm
Tired o' this city street.
Goin' back to Georgia where
That red clay can't be beat.

I want to tramp in the red mud, Lawd, and
Feel the red clay round my toes.
I want to wade in that red mud,
Feel that red clay suckin' at my toes.
I want my little farm back and I
Don't care where that landlord goes.

I want to be in Georgia, when the
Big storm starts to blow.
Yes, I want to be in Georgia when that
Big storm starts to blow.
I want to see the landlords runnin' cause I
Wonder where they gonna go!

I got them red clay blues.

How Thin a Blanket

There is so much misery in the world,
So much poverty and pain,
So many who have no food
Nor shelter from the rain,
So many wandering friendless,
So many facing cold,
So many gnawing bitter bread
And growing old!

What can I do?
And you?
What can we do alone?
How short a way
The few spare crumbs
We have will go!
How short a reach
The hand stretched out
To those who know
No handshake anywhere.
How little help our love
When they themselves
No longer care.

How thin a blanket ours
For the withered body
Of despair!

Comment on War

Let us kill off youth
For the sake of *truth*.

We who are old know what truth is—
Truth is a bundle of vicious lies
Tied together and sterilized—
A war-makers' bait for unwise youth
To kill off each other
For the sake of
Truth.

Ballad of the Miser

He took all his money
And put it in a sock
Till that sock got full
Then he got another sock.
He put all the sox
In a safe place
Behind the bricks
In the fireplace.
He worked and schemed
To stash all he could
And went around in rags
Like a beggar would.
When he died he didn't
Will a thing to anyone—

To a miser saving money's
Too much fun.

Ballad of Little Sallie

Little Sallie, Little Sallie,
I've tried every way I know
To make you like me, Little Sallie,
Now I guess I'll go.

Listen, Jimmy, listen!
You mean you're gone for good?

Little Sallie, I mean always.
I've stood all a good man could.

Then wait a minute, Jimmy.
I want you to stay.
If you went off and left me
You'd take my heart away.

Little Sallie, Little Sallie,
Then I'll marry you.
We'll put one and one together—
To make three instead of two.

That's what we'll do!

Index of First Lines

Index of Titles